The Rise of the Reich
By the SS Main Office

THE RISE OF THE REICH
SS MAIN OFFICE

Translated and annotated by Germain Muller

ANTELOPE HILL PUBLISHING

Originally published in German as *Der Weg Zum Reich* by the SS
Main Office.

Cover art by Swifty.
Edited by Harlan Wallace.
Proofread by Sebastian Durant.
Translated by Germain Muller.
Interior formatting by S. Alexander.

Antelope Hill Publishing | antelopehillpublishing.com
Paperback ISBN-13: 979-8-89252-053-9
EPUB ISBN-13: 979-8-89252-054-6

TABLE OF CONTENTS

LIST OF MAPS

TRANSLATOR'S INTRODUCTION

The work before you is more than a historical document; it is a view into an ideology that shaped one of the most significant periods of the modern era. Translating this text required a deliberate and methodical approach, balancing a commitment to linguistic fidelity with a profound understanding of its historical and ideological context. The translator's objective has been to render its rhetoric and nuance into English with precision, thereby providing the reader with an insightful view of its substance.

The Rise of the Reich is a work of general German history interpreted through a National Socialist lens, published in late 1941 (sometime after September, but before December when the United States joined the war) by the SS Main Office. It employs a particularly sophisticated yet straightforward articulation of the National Socialist worldview, as it seamlessly interweaves historical narratives, cultural achievements and political philosophy to present a cogent argument for the inevitability of the Third Reich's ascendancy. At its core, the work seeks to establish a belief in German destiny, intertwining the historical suffering and triumph that led to the National Socialist state as the ultimate culmination of the German people's historical journey.

The need for legitimation was evidently particularly high in

National Socialist historiography, as it was necessary to clearly and convincingly demonstrate that German history had been heading toward the Third Reich since the times of the Germanic tribes and was being fulfilled in it. The National Socialist Reich thus did not represent a break with history but, on the contrary, was anchored in a distant past and was the true heir of German history.

The act of translating this text was not undertaken lightly. Its content is vast, its aims ambitious, and its impact historic. Yet, to take up an ideology, one ought to first understand it in its totality. This translation is offered as a tool for analysis and education, enabling activists, scholars, and readers alike to grasp its premises and contemplate its arguments. In that spirit, the translator's role is not merely to reproduce words but to bring to life the ideas they seek to convey—to acquaint the reader with the historical and ideological underpinnings of National Socialism.

Overview of the Work

The Rise of the Reich stands clearly as both a testament to the German spirit and a clarion call for its leadership in Europe and beyond. The narrative of the text exemplifies the apotheosis of historical inevitability and the ultimate realization of a people's purpose. With its meticulous weaving of history and ideological clarity, the text functions as both a historical review and a vindication, portraying the German nation as a racial and cultural entity singularly destined to shape the course of human civilization.

At the core of the text is the thesis that the German nation, the Volk, is not merely one among many but a providential force endowed by history and nature with unique spiritual, cultural, and racial qualities that necessitate its leadership. This framing aligns with a teleological interpretation of history wherein the German race, defined in explicitly Nordic terms, has been shaped by trials and triumphs to become the natural leader of Europe. The narrative frequently invokes themes of fate, survival, and renewal to emphasize that the Reich is not a political construction, but the fulfillment of a historical mission.

The emphasis on the principles of *Blut und Boden* further strengthens this narrative. By portraying German land as an integral part of the Volk's identity, the text ties the nation's spiritual and racial essence to its geographical and agricultural roots, while the Reich is the manifestation of the Volk's spirit, sustained and justified by its national mission. Put together, this intrinsic connection between people and land provides the ideological rationale for *Lebensraum* and the exclusion of foreign elements incompatible with the racial purity of the German state.

The text grounds these ideological principles in a meticulously crafted unbroken arc of historical continuity, portraying the German journey as a series of crucibles that tested the Volk's resolve with internal disunity and external opposition and ultimately refined its identity. From the devastations of the Thirty Years' War and the Napoleonic Wars to the humiliation of the Treaty of Versailles, each hardship is positioned as a necessary prelude to renewal, which was only made possible by the Volk's racial and territorial interconnection. These trials are juxtaposed with moments of strength and unity, most notably under Bismarck and Hitler, to suggest that Germany's ascendancy and then-current lead in the Second World War are both well-deserved and preordained.

The ideological response of the Germans to these historical challenges is unity, both within the Volk and between the Volk and its leadership, which the text elevates as paramount. The *Führerprinzip* is presented as the natural and essential model of governance for a people as uniquely gifted as the Germans. The Führer, Adolf Hitler, is depicted as the personification of the Volk's collective will and destiny, a leader whose vision and resolve have brought Germany back from the brink of destruction to its rightful place of prominence.

The Führer's service to the Reich and to his Volk is marked by sacrifice and duty. The German sense of sacrifice is similarly glorified; it is tied closely to the mythos of the "unknown soldier" who symbolizes the shared suffering of the Volk in times of war and hardship. The narrative reinforces the notion that individual lives gain meaning only through their contribution to the Reich, framing personal service and sacrifice for the nation as the highest virtue.

Every sacrifice would be in vain without a racially pure Volk. Therefore, one theme most essential to the text's vision is the imperative to preserve and cultivate racial purity. It is not only a biological necessity but also a moral and spiritual duty. Statutes such as the Ancestral Estate Law and the Law for the Prevention of Hereditarily Diseased Offspring are pivotal in securing the racial integrity of the Volk. Such legislative efforts are praised as cornerstones of a racial policy that prioritizes the protection and well-being of future generations.

The safeguarding of racial purity finds its institutional counterpart in the *Schutzstaffel*, whose mission embodies both the ideological and martial dimensions of the Volk's historical role. The *Schutzstaffel*, symbolized by the *Fackel und Schwert*—allegories of ideological clarity and martial strength—represents the unity of spiritual conviction and military power, positioning itself as the vanguard of Germany's calling in world history. This duality accentuates the belief that the survival and triumph of the Reich depend on a synthesis of ideology and might.

While the *Schutzstaffel* defends the Reich's ideological and physical integrity, the text identifies the Volk's historical and contemporary enemies that jeopardize its survival. A key element of the text is its portrayal of those enemies, including France, Great Britain and Judeo-Bolshevism. These perennial threats are portrayed as existential challenges that necessitate Germany's rise to power. The narrative suggests that Germany's expansion—whether through the *Anschluss*, the reclamation of the lost eastern territories or the establishment of the *Neuordnung* in Europe—is not only warranted but indispensable to the survival of Western civilization itself.

This reasoning is reinforced by the depiction of the Treaty of Versailles as a *Schanddiktat* (a disgraceful treaty unilaterally imposed on a downed Germany), along with emphasis on the injustices suffered by the German Volk after the First World War. By citing Versailles as the prime example of the foreign conspiracies designed to subjugate Germany, the text builds a moral case for its reaction as both victim and avenger, including rearmament, territorial expansion and the unification of all German-speaking peoples under the Reich, all of which are meant to serve its role as a European leader.

German cultural achievements—from the Reformation to the oeuvre of Beethoven to the philosophy of Kant—serve to bolster the claim that Germany is uniquely qualified to lead Europe. The concept of German leadership is in the fulfillment of a natural and benevolent responsibility to Germany's European brothers.

This idea of leadership is explicitly contrasted with the exploitative colonial practices of other European powers, particularly the British Empire. By depicting German expansion as a mission of cultural and racial renewal rather than conquest, the text seeks to present the Reich's actions as a historically necessary moral imperative, informed by the ideology of National Socialism.

Having established the historical context, the text shifts focus to the ideological tenets that underpin National Socialist thought. National Socialism is presented as the summit of Germany's historical development and the only political system capable of fulfilling the Volk's destiny. Its emphasis on the *Volksgemeinschaft*, self-sacrifice and racial purity is the antidote to the decadence and individualism of liberal democracy and the chaos of Marxism. By uniting the Volk under a single world view and leadership, National Socialism was able to create a state that is both efficient and spiritually meaningful.

The symbiotic relationship between the National Socialist world view and the German state is underscored by the NSDAP's role as the "living conscience" of the Volk and the instrument through which the Führer's vision is realized. This harmony is considered the key to the rise of the German Reich.

As these historical and ideological threads coalesce, the work concludes with an almost religious conviction in the inevitability and righteousness of the rise of the Reich. By describing the Third Reich as the "natural" consummation of Germany's historical, racial and cultural forces, it seeks to inspire fervent loyalty, a sense of sacrifice and unwavering faith in the National Socialist vision. It leaves no room for doubt: The German Volk, under the guidance of the Führer, has overcome centuries of division and opposition to satisfy its *raison d'être* as the leader of Europe and the guardian of Western civilization.

For Today's Reader

To read the present text is to peer into history and engage the ideology of National Socialism. The book's language is crafted to inspire and galvanize, to provide a sense of purpose and destiny to a people. It is precisely this uplifting resolve that the West needs most today. By examining its content, we not only better understand the history of many of our brothers and sisters in our collective struggle, but we also better understand the history of the struggle itself. Let this work serve as a reminder of the power and importance of our shared zeal. As you delve into the book, do so with the resolve to restore our heritage and secure a bright future for our posterity.

Germain Muller
2025

CHAPTER ONE: ANCIENT GERMAN HISTORY

Do the events of the past five millennia hold any significance for us today? Is it not enough to see ourselves as a people living in the present? Does looking back on the past not imply feeble elderliness?

Certainly not. We know today that we are all just a link in the chain of the bloodline of our ancestors, which proceeds from the infinite past into the infinite future. Ensuring this bloodline never runs dry is the solemn task of each generation. Conversant with racial anthropology, our National Socialist worldview teaches that a people's genotype found in pure blood remains uncorrupted over millennia. Therefore, awareness of history is awareness of oneself. It is knowledge of one's own kind, of its potential for development, its faults and weaknesses; it means openness to the call of the blood as a prerequisite for the general understanding of the fateful mission of one's own people.

Throughout history, we see that nations in times of awakening and ascent draw their greatest strengths from the example of the past. For example, the liberation of the Greeks from Turkish rule a century ago led to a strong renewal of their ancient heritage.[1] Mussolini also consciously built the new Italy on the foundations of ancient Rome. Despite adopting many technological innovations from Europe, the Japanese have similarly remained faithful to their own traditions.

And the new Reich, whose dawn we are witnessing, is rebuilding the nation on the foundations of its life and its mission after decades of decline and deterioration. We now understand why the leaders of the new state repeatedly emphasize the ancient history of our people as the bedrock of this renewal.

Legends and Songs Among the Ancient Germans

The ancient Germanic peoples carefully preserved their traditions, passing down their legends and songs not only orally but also in written form. Memories of significant events from Germanic times have even survived to this day in sagas and fairy tales. Few realize that our forefathers would sit by the hearth and tell stories just as our grandparents do today. Rural communities still retain a rich treasure of Germanic heritage in their songs, poems, proverbs, legends, fables, anecdotes, children's games, and nursery rhymes.

For example, the *Schimmelreiter*,[2] a traditional figure during the Christmas season, mirrors the figure of Odin in folk belief.[3]

---

[1] Most of the territory of modern Greece was once part of the Ottoman Empire. Ottoman rule in Greece spanned from the mid-fifteenth century until the Greek War of Independence, from 1821 to 1829. The revolution ultimately led to the proclamation of the First Hellenic Republic.

[2] In Germanic legend, the *Schimmelreiter* is a ghostly rider on a white horse who races through the air at the head of an army of ghosts on stormy nights near the winter solstice.

[3] Odin or Wotan is a key figure in Germanic mythology. While his exact characterization has varied between times and places, he is traditionally associated with magic, poetry, warfare, and frenzy, and commonly identified as the chief deity in the Germanic pantheon, as portrayed most famously in Wagner's operas.

Another Christmas figure is Frau Holle, Frau Harke, or Frau Perchta—often associated with a spindle.[4] Similar to the wise women in the fairy tale of the Sleeping Beauty,[5] the legend of the three Norns also lives on, who in Nordic tradition bring a newborn child his life's destiny as a "gift."[6] In folk belief, the Norns still spin threads to this day, which are chanced upon as gossamer.[7] In Bavaria, these threads are tellingly attributed to the Virgin Mary. The fact that the ancient Germanic peoples not only had oral traditions but also written ones can be inferred from the runic alphabets of the Stone Age, but also from symbolic images and rune stones.

Why Do We Know So Little About Ancient German History?

If today we must laboriously search through Germanic antiquity, finding it so difficult to research the life and activities, the battles and struggles of the Germanic peoples, it is because early in the Middle Ages, Germanic traditions were deliberately and artificially destroyed. Only misunderstood remnants, often misinterpreted by opponents, shine faintly through the heavy cloak of Christianity in the art and customs of the peasantry, in

---

[4] Frau Holle, Frau Harke, and Frau Perchta more or less refer to the same legendary figure. She is commonly depicted as a benevolent old woman who shakes out her down pillows in heaven, with the loose feathers falling to earth as snow.

[5] In anglophone countries, most would be familiar with the tale of the Sleeping Beauty including three fairies; however, in the Germanic rendition of the folktale (as recorded by the Brothers Grimm), the fairies are replaced by three wise women.

[6] The Norns are the three virgin goddesses of destiny in Germanic mythology who spin the thread of fate.

[7] Gossamer are fine strands of cobwebs that are often found floating in the air or caught on tree branches.

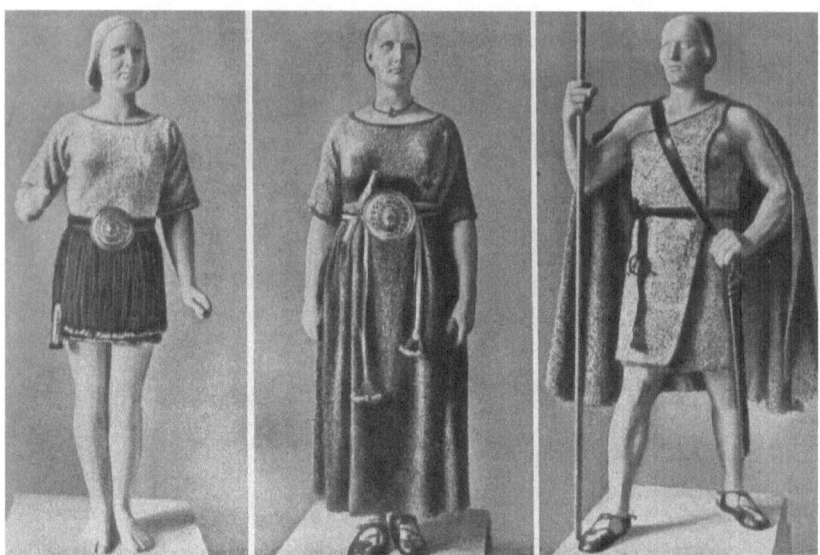

The oldest complete garments in the world are Germanic. These are faithfully recreated replicas of Germanic attire from the Bronze Age, dating back more than three millennia.

Christmas and St. John's fire.[8] The wisdom of our ancestors was supplanted by an alien tradition. This is particularly evident in the laws promulgated by Charlemagne after his campaign against the Saxons.[9] Charlemagne collected any Germanic writings that were found and replaced the local customs with Latin liturgy. His son Louis, whom the grateful Church called "the Pious," went so far in his Christian zeal that he burned the Germanic heroic lays collected by his father.[10] After that, maybe one could then

---

[8] St. John's fire is an outdoor bonfire lit as part of a festival on the night before St. John's Day, a holiday dedicated to St. John the Baptist observed annually on June 24th. Pre-Christian Nordic countries celebrated the day as a summer solstice festival with no connection to the saint.

[9] Charlemagne was a Frankish king and ruler of what is now known as the Carolingian Empire. His eighth-century battle with the Saxons is referred to as the Saxon Wars, in which the Franks under Charlemagne sought to conquer Saxony and convert the populace to Christianity. The Saxons would ultimately lose.

[10] A heroic lay is a form of epic poetry (usually from the fifth to eighth centuries AD), the material of which is taken from Germanic heroic legends.

Map 1: Largest versus Latest Glaciation

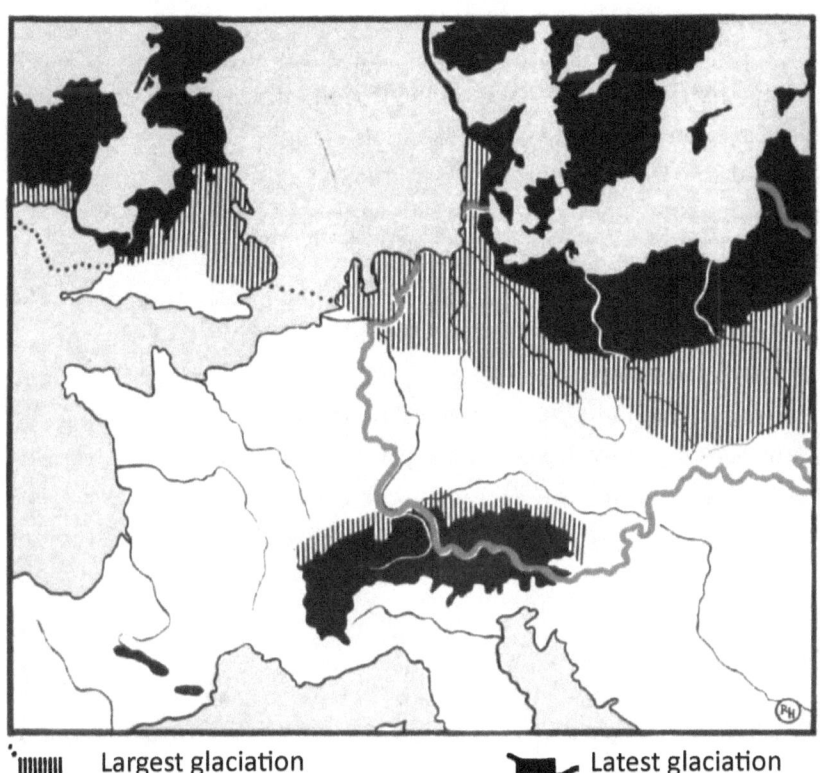

ılılılılı Largest glaciation   Latest glaciation

As a result of a significant worsening of the climate, a severe glaciation occurred in Europe. Massive ice sheets from Scandinavia pushed across the North and Baltic Seas. All life was forced to retreat to the areas that remained ice-free or else be buried under a cover of ice, often one kilometer thick.

The center of the second glaciation was the Alps. From there, large ice fronts advanced far. The Salzach and Inn glaciers reached as far as Braunau am Inn, and the Isar-Loisach glacier almost extended as far as Munich. Even today, we see evidence of this former glaciation in Northern Germany in the form of glacial erratics (massive rocks that were carried there by glaciers from Scandinavia).

Variations in the climate repeatedly caused the glaciers to retreat and advance again; these intervals are known as interglacial periods. Only after the glacial period had finally subsided were the northern regions suitable for permanent habitation by plants, animals, and humans.

shamelessly claim that the Germanic peoples had no written tradition at all.

Bereft of any sense of identity, German "scholars" gazed toward the south, transfixed, believing all culture originated there. Not so long ago, German schools taught that the barbaric Germanic tribes vandalized the marvelous cultural treasures of the south during their conquests, but ultimately submitted to the superior Roman culture.[11] Only then did the light of culture penetrate the dark forests of Germania; only then did the Germanic tribes evolve from a wild, primitive people into a civilized society. Just as centuries past coined the phrase "from the east comes the light,"[12] we now say, after meticulously tracing the paths of our ancestors, which prove that cultural innovations belong to the north: "From the north comes strength." No amount of foreign interference could prevent the rediscovery of our ancient Germanic history.

Germania By Tacitus

From the brief book titled the *Germania* by the ancient Roman historian Tacitus, first discovered around the time of Luther, various things about our ancestors were revealed.

However, none of these efforts led to the rebirth of our ancient past, because the bridge to it had been dismantled by a foreign civilization. We viewed our forefathers only through the

---

[11] The English word "vandalize" comes from the term "vandal," which actually refers to the ancient Germanic peoples known as the Vandals, who were said to be senselessly destructive during the Sack of Rome in 455. During the Enlightenment, Rome was idealized, while the Goths and Vandals were blamed for its destruction. Today, we know that the Vandals were no more destructive than any other invaders of ancient times, including the Romans themselves.

[12] The original adage is in Latin (*ex oriente lux*), and it most literally refers to the sun rising in the east; however, it has been extended in various ways to refer, for example, to Christianity coming to Europe from the east, or to the hypothesis that human civilization began in the Middle East.

eyes of an alien, that is to say, the Roman, to whom we owed the only—often misleading and malicious—accounts of our forebears. The uncompromising testimony of archaeology had not yet been understood, and so the attempts of that time to reconnect with our ancient past were doomed to fail from the outset.

Wars of Liberation as an Impetus for German Prehistoric Studies

Only through the enthusiasm sparked by the Wars of Liberation was German prehistoric studies revived as a truly scientific discipline.[13] The voices claiming that the Germanic tribesman was some beast of prey who spent his waking hours doing nothing but hunting, drinking, and eating grew increasingly rare. It became recognized that the former line of research had been mistaken.

Brothers Grimm

Our ancient culture, true to itself, was now eagerly explored. The Brothers Grimm established connections between the laws, language, fairy tales, and sagas of early Germany. It was understood that all the previously researched artifacts were not mere curiosities admired for their peculiar nature, but that they represented records of the earliest development of our ancestors. From these findings, it was deduced that the earliest stage was the Stone Age, followed by the Bronze Age, and finally the Iron Age —three periods of human development.[14] Based on his excavations, the German researcher Lisch recognized the cultural superiority of the Bronze Age Germanic peoples compared to the

---

[13] The Wars of Liberation were a series of battles from 1813 to 1815 that liberated Germany (and most of Europe) from Napoleon's rule.

[14] This tripartite division of prehistory is known as the three-age system, and it remains the basis of prehistoric Eurasian chronology.

southern peoples living at the same time.[15] It is also no coincidence that he was the first to draw attention to the swastikas engraved on Germanic clay urns, attributing a "sacred significance" to them.

Just as the burgeoning German consciousness was unceremoniously suppressed by the reactionary forces in the mid-nineteenth century—when Jews, Freemasons, and Christian churches aligned themselves—so too were the promising beginnings of German prehistoric research destroyed by obsolete humanist scholarship, which sought refuge in the south. It was once again claimed that the Germanic peoples were stuck in the Stone Age until the Roman era, that the magnificent bronze works of art of the north were all imported from Mediterranean lands. Some even believed they could identify Italian merchants in the tree-trunk coffins of Jutland, dressed in their elegant wool attire;[16] Germanics, of course, could only adorn themselves with crude furs and massive wooden clubs!

Father of Prehistoric Studies

These views about our earliest ancestors, which seem scarcely credible to us today, were widely accepted in Germany when Gustaf Kossinna began his quest to reclaim our prehistory. He opened his seminal book, *German Prehistory: A Pre-Eminently National Discipline*, with Jacob Grimm's words: "Because I learned that its language, its law, and its history were

---

[15] Georg Christian Friedrich Lisch was a German archaeologist and prehistorian. He is considered one of the most important German historians of the nineteenth century.

[16] A tree-trunk coffin is a coffin hollowed out of a single large log, often used in prehistoric burial rituals of Northern Europe. Jutland is a peninsula in Northwestern Europe, forming the mainland of Denmark and the Northern German state of Schleswig-Holstein.

undervalued, I wanted to elevate my fatherland."[17] In 1895, Kossinna precisely defined the earliest areas of settlement of the Germanic peoples. Later, he also demonstrated the Nordic origin of the Indo-Europeans, the family of peoples to which the Germanic tribes belong. This unmistakably proved that Germany and the Nordic race had been at the center of European history since the earliest times.

---

[17] Jacob Grimm, *Deutsche Mythologie* ["German Mythology"], 2nd ed., vol. 1, p. xlviii (Göttingen: Dieterichsche Buchhandlung, 1844).

CHAPTER TWO: STRENGTH FROM THE NORTH

Nordics in the Neolithic Around 3000 to 1800 BC[18]

Humans During the Ice Age

We know little about the earliest beginnings of settlement in our fatherland, as glaciation and erosion have destroyed and covered their traces. In repeated advances, the masses of ice from Scandinavia reached the mountain ranges of Central Germany, and from the Alps, they extended beyond the Danube. (See Map 1.)

It was not until the last Ice Age, many tens of thousands of years ago, that we could clearly identify the primitive forms of today's European races, especially the Nordic race. Perhaps the pressures of natural selection from living at the edge of the Scandinavian glaciers contributed then to the formation of the Nordic race.

---

[18] The Neolithic period began around 10,000 BC and marked the transition from nomadic hunter-gatherer communities to settled agricultural societies. This era saw the domestication of plants and animals, leading to the establishment of permanent settlements and advancements in tools and pottery. The Neolithic laid the foundation for early civilization and witnessed significant cultural and technological progress.

Nordic Heartland

Toward the end of the Paleolithic, around 10,000 BC, the glaciers finally melted.[19] The climate became milder, and the north became dry and suitable for plant growth. Consequently, the North German and South Scandinavian regions became permanently suitable for human habitation. This area became the heartland of the Nordic race, which was to play a decisive role in the formation of our people. Here lies the origin of our people.

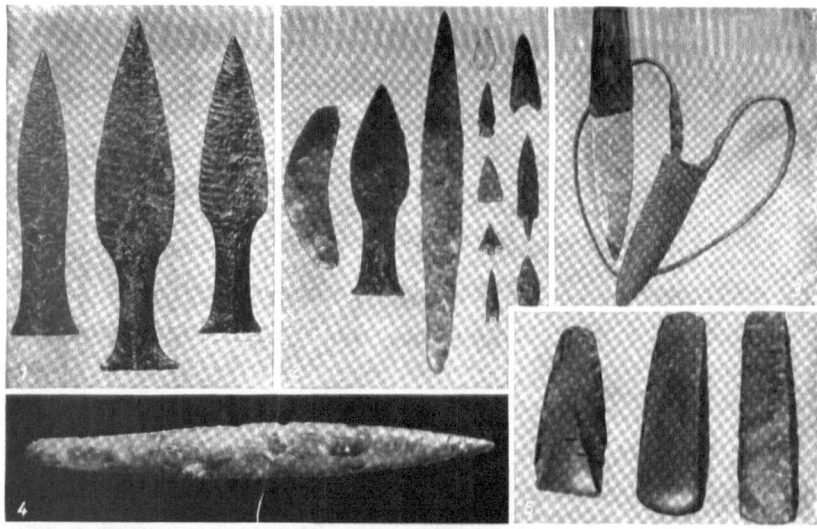

Weapons and tools from the Neolithic period

1. Hilted daggers 2. Flint sickles, daggers and arrowheads 3. A flint dagger with a wooden handle and leather sheath 4. A long dagger 5. Polished flint axes

---

[19] The Paleolithic period spanned from approximately 2.5 million years ago to the end of the last Ice Age (around 10,000 BC). It was characterized by the use of simple stone tools and a hunter-gatherer lifestyle, with humans living in small, nomadic groups. This era saw the development of hand tools, such as the axe. It was the era of the Neanderthal man and saw the eventual emergence of modern *Homo sapiens*.

The towering memorials of the Germanic tribes for their dead, inseparably linked to their clans, stood prominently visible far and wide.

Nordic Way of Life

Of course, it was not only the Nordic man who initially settled in Northern Germany. Gradually, however, the superiority of the Nordic (warlike) and the related Dalo-Falid (peaceful) races became evident in their struggle in the wilderness of the Nordic lands.[20] From the very beginning, the Nordic way of life proved far superior to the other cultures forming in Europe around the same time. The bearers of this Nordic culture were the immediate ancestors of the Germanic peoples. We can refer to them as proto-Germanic, Aryan, or Indo-European—a term coined for the original ancestors of all the peoples that speak related languages which span from India, through the Middle East, into Spain and

---

[20] While many are familiar with the concept of the Nordic race, the Dalo-Falid race was believed to be especially numerous in Westphalia (Northwestern Germany) and was first identified by German ethnologist Fritz Paudler in Dalarna (Central Sweden) in 1924. Despite being called "races," these terms refer not so much to unique races as they do to physical categorizations of different ethnicities in Europe.

up to the Germanic lands of the north.

Barrows

"German history does not begin with Charlemagne but with the barrows of the heath,"[21] Alfred Rosenberg once said.[22] The re-evaluation of German history, seen anew in the light of racial

A glimpse into life during the Neolithic

The rectangular house and the plow originated in the Nordic region and spread to the rest of the world.

---

[21] A barrow is an ancient megalithic burial mound. A heath is an area of open uncultivated land with poor sandy soil, typically covered with low vegetation such as heather and gorse; it is commonly found in regions with temperate climates, particularly in parts of Europe, and is not common in the Americas.

[22] As quoted by Rudolf Ströbel, *Unseres Volkes Ursprung: 5000 Jahre nordisch-germanische Kulturentwicklung* ["Our People's Origin: 5,000 Years of Nordic-Germanic Cultural Development"], p. 6 (Berlin: Propaganda-Verlag, 1935).

research, did not stop at Emperor Charlemagne but extended the history of the German people back thousands of years by including prehistory. The Germanic mythos, not Christianity, stands at the beginning of German history. The decisive factor in our view of history is the power of our blood, which has formed the German people from the time of the Germanic tribes to the present day.

At the sight of these massive stone tombs, no one can escape the feeling of deep reverence for our ancient history. The dead resting in those barrows belong to the Nordic and particularly the Dalo-Falid race. The weapons found within show an artistic style that resonates with us to this day. This ancient Nordic people must have been very technically skilled to produce these excellent weapons and tools but especially to build the tombs themselves. Without cranes and machinery, using only a ramp built from dirt, they managed to stack massive blocks of rock weighing up to fifty thousand pounds using only levers and wheels. These structures could only have been erected through the organized cooperation of a large community. Thus, as early as 3000 BC, there must have been a state-like cohesion among our ancestors.

Nordic Funerary Beliefs

These megalithic tombs also testify to the profound nature of Nordic funerary beliefs. The concept of a separation between body and soul was initially unknown in the Stone Age, even in the north, yet this ancient belief contains a profound truth: There are unfathomably deep connections between body and soul that transmit from generation to generation. Since people in the Stone Age conceived of an afterlife in physical terms, they lovingly cared for their dead by building them an enduring house and providing them with everything they would need after death.

By the end of the Neolithic in the north, belief in the soul—a belief in a new, different life after death—had completely

Map 2: Conquest and Settlement of the Nordic Indo-
Europeans around 3000 to 1800 BC

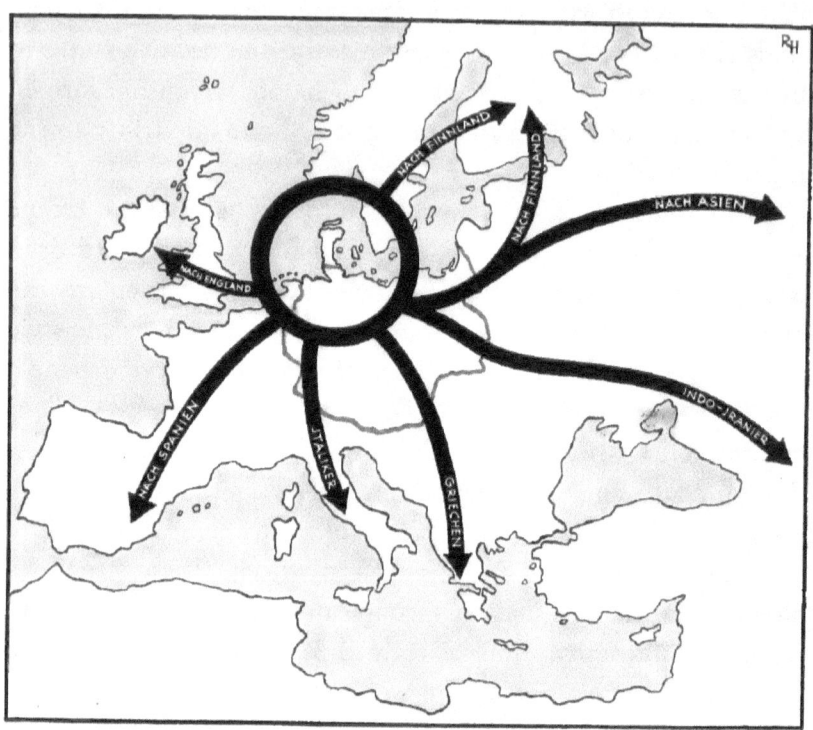

From the Nordic heartland, blond tribes from the regions around the North and
Baltic Seas began migrating south, east and west about five thousand years ago,
leaving behind traces of their culture everywhere. They thus established the Aryan
culture of India and laid the groundwork for the rise of Persia. Nordic blood also
shaped the cultures of Greece and the Roman Empire.

supplanted the old belief in the continuing physical existence of the
deceased. This is evidenced by the emerging practice of cremation.
Preserving the body had become unnecessary; through cremation,
the soul was freed from the last remnants of bodily existence. It was
only under the foreign influences of the post-Christian periods that
the Germanic peoples partially resumed the practice of interment.

The people of this culture left us not only these massive
memorials to the dead, with arrangements of stone reaching up to

one hundred meters in length, but also beautifully crafted pottery vessels and finely polished battle axes and daggers.

Nordic Man as Farmer

The Nordics of the Neolithic era were settled and, alongside their proclivity for hunting, had developed a fully-fledged agrarian culture.

This is evidenced by archaeologists' discovery of the plows (which spread from this region throughout the world), as well as various types of grain, horses, wagons, and the Nordic rectangular house.[23] This style of house would later emerge during the Indo-European migrations wherever the Nordic people settled.

Toward the end of the late Neolithic, as the climate became drier, the vast migrations of the Nordic peoples began in several waves, primarily moving eastward. (See Map 2.) As farmers, they needed new fields and pastures for their posterity. However, these migratory patterns also reveal traits of a warrior race, one with a daring entrepreneurial spirit and a drive for colonization and territorial expansion.

Indo-Europeans

These Northmen, equated with Indo-Europeans or Aryans, spread across almost all of Europe and large parts of Asia. The westward migration reached as far as Britain and Spain. The southward migration crossed the Gotthard Pass into Italy.[24] In the southeast,

---

[23] The so-called rectangular house is considered an advancement in Neolithic architecture that offered more advantages over the more primitive circular house. It, for example, allowed the builder to construct it of wood and brick more easily, and it was easier to create rooms within it or add expansions later. They were more notable among agrarian cultures.

[24] The Gotthard Pass, located in the Swiss Alps, has been a crucial transit route since European prehistory, facilitating movement and trade between Northern and Southern Europe.

Map 3: Original Site of the Germanic Peoples and Presumed
Sites of the Different Indo-European Peoples

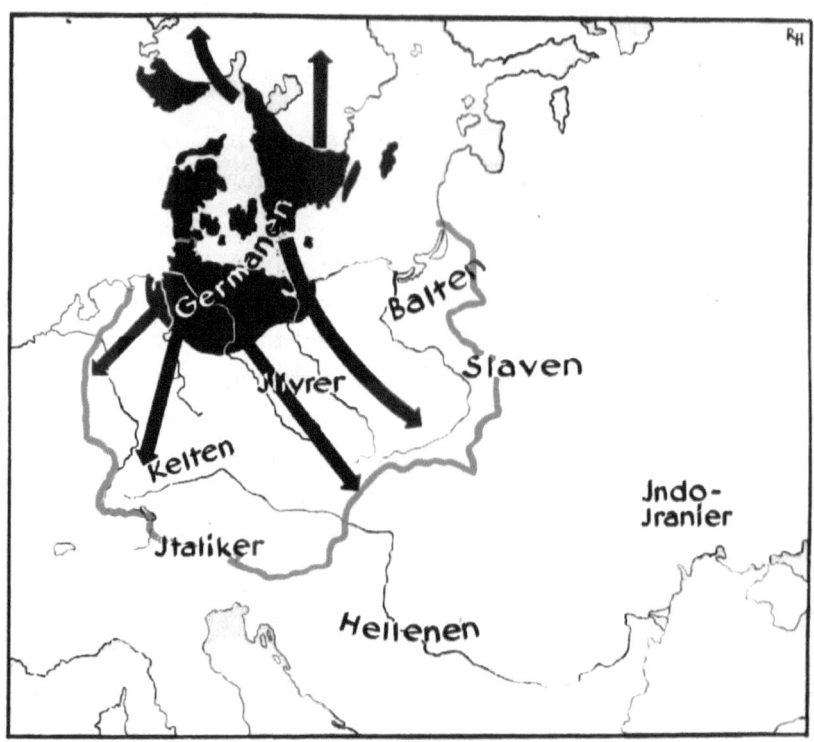

Around 2000 bc, the Germanic peoples inhabited the following areas: Southern
Scandinavia, Jutland, the Danish islands, and the regions around the North and
Baltic Seas, with the southern border roughly at the Thuringian Forest. From this
heartland, the Germanic peoples later advanced further north and into the territories
of the Celts, the Illyrians, and others.

the Indo-Europeans pushed through Bohemia and Moravia into
Hungary and Transylvania, and from there into Greece. But the
most impressive triumph was the eastern conquest: Through Poland
and Southern Russia, they moved across the Caucasus into Persia
and India, reaching as far as Southeast Asia and Japan. In the
northeast, Finland and large parts of Russia up to the Ural
Mountains and Northeastern Siberia were settled.

Nordic Indo-European Culture as Unifying Force of Europe

The expansion of the Nordic Indo-Europeans completely reshaped Europe. Most of today's European nations trace their distant roots back to this common Indo-European heritage.

From this single origin emerged the Germanic, Celtic, Slavic, Baltic, Italic, Greek, Persian, and Indian peoples, among others. It is interesting to note that the cultural golden age of all these nations began with the arrival of the Nordic Indo-Europeans. The high cultures of these peoples declined whenever the Nordic ruling class grew soft from a southern climate and mixed excessively with the indigenous populations of the south, west, and east, such as in India, Persia, Greece, and Rome. Contrary to what earlier historical research suggested, the Germanic peoples of this migratory period did not destroy the ancient cultures of the south; rather, they revived the Nordic foundation of Europe from its deathbed, thereby creating modern Europe.

Germanic Peoples

Heartland of the Germanic Peoples

Nonetheless, a portion of the Indo-Europeans remained in the Nordic heartland and did not mix with foreign blood; these were the Germanic peoples. Starting with the end of the Indo-European migrations and the beginning of the Bronze Age (1800 to 800 BC), they are referred to as Germanic. They once again occupied the same region along the coasts of the North and Baltic Seas where the Indo-Europeans had lived before their migrations began. (See Map 3.)

The Germanic peoples are, therefore, the only pure descendants of the Nordic Indo-Europeans. Those who, according to the old theory, were considered the last European people to be blessed with a higher culture are actually the trunk of the tree of European nations. It is no wonder the Germanic peoples proved superior to the surrounding mixed populations, continually imparting new blood and cultural treasures to them.

Cultural Flourishing in the Bronze Age

The first period of Germanic development, the Bronze Age, is not marked by aggression and conflict. Instead, following the loss of blood due to the Indo-European migrations, it represents a time of peaceful maturation leading to an unprecedented flourishing of culture.

The Germanic peoples produced unparalleled masterpieces of bronze casting. Bronze, an alloy of nine parts copper to one part tin, was already being mined and smelted by the Nordic Indo-Europeans as early as the end of the Neolithic. One of the oldest and most important copper-producing regions is Central Germany; from there and the Eastern Alps, the Germanic peoples sourced their copper and tin for the new metal. The design of stone tools was initially reproduced in the new material, which strongly demonstrates that the Germanic peoples independently developed their bronze-working techniques; only gradually did they achieve the level of perfection in design and embellishment that we today admire in Germanic works of bronze.

Wood as a Raw Material

Despite the refined metalworking, wood became the foundation of Germanic craftsmanship. Unfortunately, very few of these wooden artifacts have survived, as wood is highly susceptible to decomposition. However, we can infer their existence from rock art. Some petroglyphs (rock carvings), for example, depict ships lined up in battle formations, with several larger vessels in the vanguard, serving as permanent testimony to the early seafaring capabilities of our Germanic ancestors.

Germanic Attire

The attire of the Germanic peoples is an expression of their inner disposition. One need only compare the Germanic peoples of thirty-five hundred years ago with the recent portrayals of them in literature and imagery, in film and theater, to see how gravely we have wronged our ancestors.

Personal Hygiene and Sport

Our ancestors valued personal hygiene and sport highly. Just like clothing, personal hygiene is an unfailing measure of their culture. Soap and steam baths were introduced to other European nations by the Germanic peoples. Men's graves from the Bronze Age always contain straight razors and tweezers for plucking hair, indicating that men were clean-shaven and wore long hair. This contradicts the notion of the unkempt beards often attributed to the Germanic peoples. It is no wonder that the Germanic peoples enjoyed engaging in sport with their healthy and well-groomed bodies. Sword dances, horse jumping, racing, shot put, and other sports have been passed down to us from later Germanic times. The chivalrous duel was the fighting style suited to the Germanic peoples.

Religious Beliefs

The religious beliefs of our ancestors centered on the sun as the symbol of life. The chief religious observances of the Germanic peoples took place at the winter and summer solstices. Those observances vividly illustrate the sophisticated culture of our ancestors. In ceremonial garb, the men, along with women and children, awaited daybreak. A tree with a woven wreath, a symbol of the sun, was erected, the now traditional solstice bonfire was lit, and the lur players greeted the sunlight with celebratory music.[25] Formal processions were also held, in which the sun chariot was carried along.[26]

The Struggle of the Germanic Peoples in the Iron Age Since 800 BC

Iron Age

With the beginning of the Late Bronze Age, a large-scale migration commenced that we might collectively refer to as Germanic settling (see Map 4); this began much earlier than the historical Migration Period starting in AD 375.[27]

This massive phenomenon involved all of Europe and eventually extended to Africa and the Americas. A thirst for action, overpopulation, and the desire for the sunny south might have driven the individual Germanic tribes to migrate. However, the beginning of the great Germanic settling was a result of a sharp decline in the climate at the end of the Bronze Age. A cold and wet period began, with average annual temperatures dropping by four degrees Fahrenheit. The land of Northern Germany and Scandinavia could no longer sustain its numerous inhabitants.

Iron, the New Metal

The worsening climate and its aftereffects increased the demand for metal tools and weapons. The supply of copper and tin faltered due to the population movements. As a result, the Germanic peoples adopted

---

[25] The solstice bonfire was a very large bonfire traditionally lit by the community to celebrate solstices. A lur is a long S-shaped trumpet.

[26] The sun was envisaged as traveling through the sky on a chariot commanded by a solar deity.

[27] The Migration Period, occurring from the fourth to the eighth century AD, was a time of significant movement and settlement of various tribes across Europe, which ultimately contributed to the decline of the Roman Empire and the reshaping of the continent's political landscape.

iron as a substitute, a material they had already been using for ornamental purposes. Because of this crisis, Germanic craftsmen quickly learned how to properly extract and work with this new material.

The Eastward Migration of the Germanic Peoples

Migration of the Vistula Germanic Tribes[28]

To reclaim the territory they lost in the aftermath of the deteriorating climate, the Germanic migration eastward began in the early Iron Age, starting in the area between the Vistula and Oder rivers. A strong Germanic tribe had formed there, which around 500 BC had entirely settled the regions of Silesia and Posen.[29] Here, these Vistula Germanic tribes encountered the Illyrians, who, after initial resistance, could not withstand the onslaught of the vigorous Germanic warriors. Some Illyrians retreated south to what we would later call Illyria,[30] while others mixed with the Germanic conquerors, who can be separated into two historical tribes: the Bastarnae (meaning "mongrels") and the Sciri (meaning "pure" or "unmixed").[31] However, their time in Eastern Germany was brief. The Germanic peoples continued to migrate as a broad front, reaching the Southern Russian coast of the Black Sea. There, they

---

[28] The Vistula Germanic tribes lived between the Vistula and Oder Rivers in modern-day Poland. Member tribes included the Vandals, the Goths and the Burgundians.

[29] Silesia and Posen are regions historically contested between the Germans, Czechs, and Poles, today making up the greater part of western Poland.

[30] Illyria is an ancient region located along the eastern coast of the Adriatic Sea, encompassing parts of what are now Croatia, Montenegro and Albania.

[31] It has been suggested that the term *Bastarnae* is linked with the Germanic word *Bastard*, meaning "mongrel." Additionally, the Sciri were a Germanic tribe who lived in the same general region, and it is likely their name means "the pure ones." However, whether *Bastarnae* actually refers to mongrels—and indeed whether the Bastarnae were Germanic at all—remains contested.

came into contact with the Greco-Roman world.

Migration From Jutland

The second wave of Germanic migration began in Jutland. In the second century BC, the Cimbri and Teutons first appeared by sea on the Baltic coast, rapidly advancing up the Oder River. They infamously struck great fear in the Romans—which has been called *terror cimbricus*—and triumphantly penetrated Roman territories.[32] However, they ultimately met a tragic end because of a lack of fresh supplies from their homeland, from which Roman cunning had cleverly separated them.

Migration of the Vandals

Another Jutland region, Vendsyssel, preserves the name of the Vandals, who originated from here and settled in Silesia, large parts of Poland, and Galicia in the first century BC.[33] They lived for centuries in their new homeland, achieving a high standard of living and great wealth. They were masters of goldsmithing and blacksmithing.

Home of the Burgundians

North of the Vandals stretched the territory of the Burgundians, who had come over to the mainland from present-day Bornholm.[34] Lavish burial sites show that they in particular were master bladesmiths.

---

[32] Together with the Teutons, the Cimbri fought the Romans during the Cimbrian War, which the Romans ultimately won. Nonetheless, the Cimbri were extremely terrifying to the ancient Romans and a state of emergency was declared after initial Roman losses in the war. The Romans referred to this mass panic as *terror cimbricus* or "the Cimbrian terror."

[33] Galicia is a region of East Central Europe, north of the Carpathian Mountains.

[34] Bornholm is a Danish island in the Baltic Sea, southeast of Sweden.

Goths and Gepids Move to the Southeast[35]

By the first century AD, the Goths and Gepids were the last East Germanic people to migrate from the Swedish regions of Östergötland and Västergötland, as well as from Gotland, across the Baltic Sea to the mouth of the Vistula.[36] Like the Bastarnae and Sciri a few centuries before them, they too migrated southeastward. The Ostrogoths founded a powerful kingdom by the Black Sea around AD 200. The Gothic language was still spoken on the Crimean Peninsula as late as the sixteenth century. The Visigoths occupied Transylvania and Wallachia, while the Gepids settled in Hungary.[37] Early on, the Rhine became a Germanic river.

Germanic Peoples on the Rhine

Just as systematically as in the east, the Germanic settlement of land proceeded in the west. By the end of the Bronze Age, around 800 BC, the Germanic peoples reached the Lower Rhine. By 500 BC, the Rhine basin as far as Bingen, and also Belgium and part of Northern France, had become Germanic. In the west, the Germanic peoples increasingly mixed with the subdued Celts and partly assimilated into Celtic culture. For example, the Celtic tribes of the Belgae proudly clung to their Germanic ancestry even in Caesar's time.

During the early Iron Age, the people of the so-called

---

[35] The Gepids were an East Germanic people who lived in the area of modern Romania, Hungary and Serbia.

[36] Östergötland and Västergötland are two regions in Southern Sweden, and Gotland is an island off the coast of Southern Sweden.

[37] Transylvania and Wallachia are large historical regions in Central Europe that today encompass much of Romania.

Map 4: Acquisition of German Territory by the Germanic
Peoples from 2000 BC to AD 1

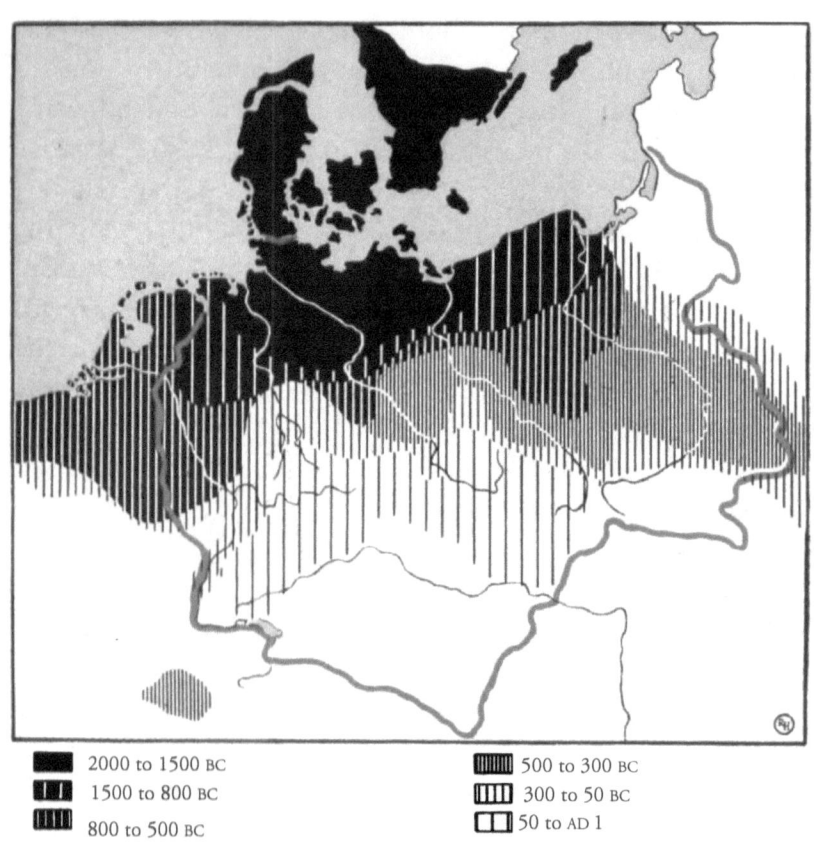

	2000 to 1500 BC		500 to 300 BC
	1500 to 800 BC		300 to 50 BC
	800 to 500 BC		50 to AD 1

The undiminished strength of the Germanic peoples established the necessary living
space for them to develop over the centuries.

Hallstatt culture resided in Southern Germany.[38] This agrarian
population was ruled by wealthy chieftains, and their beautifully
decorated and brightly painted pear-shaped vases are
particularly notable. However, even the fortified castles of their

---

[38] The Hallstatt culture, flourishing from approximately 800 to 450 BC in
Central Europe, is notable for its advanced metalworking, reliance on
agriculture and extensive trade networks.

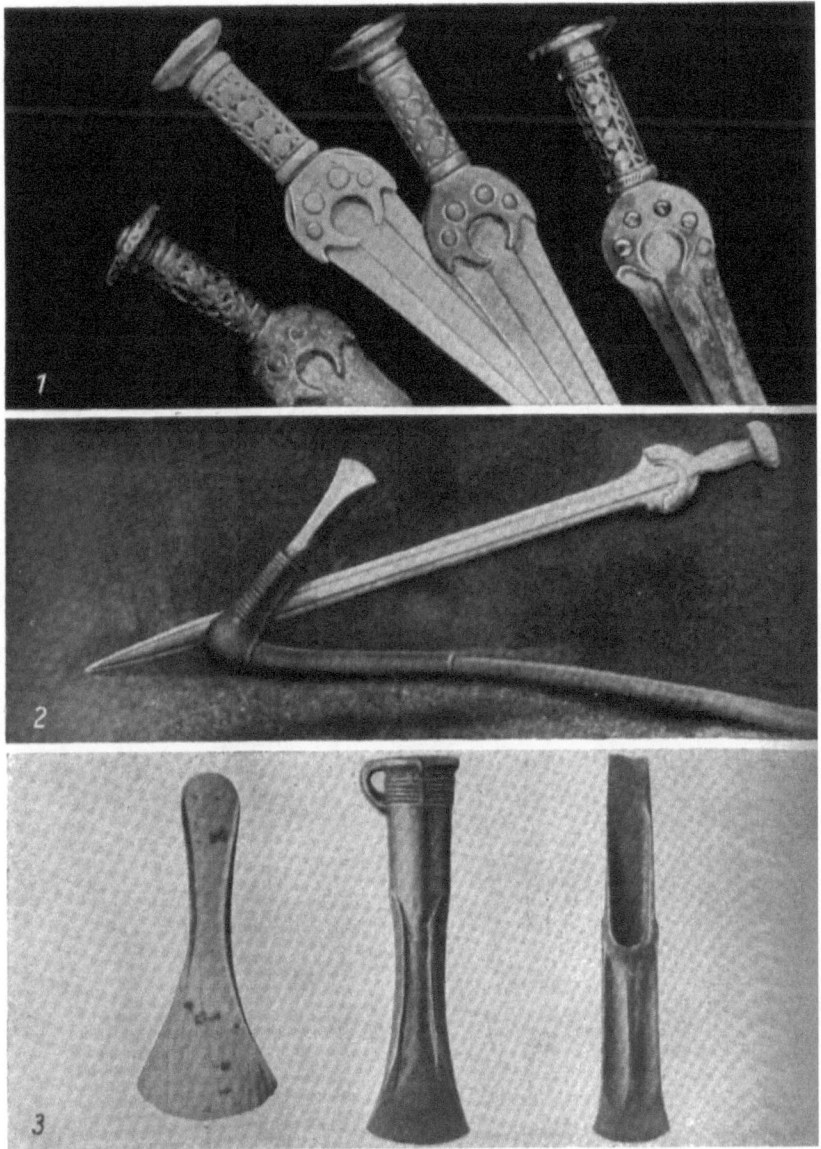

Bronze tools and weapons from three thousand years ago

1. Several bronze swords 2. A longsword and battle axe 3. Bronze axe heads

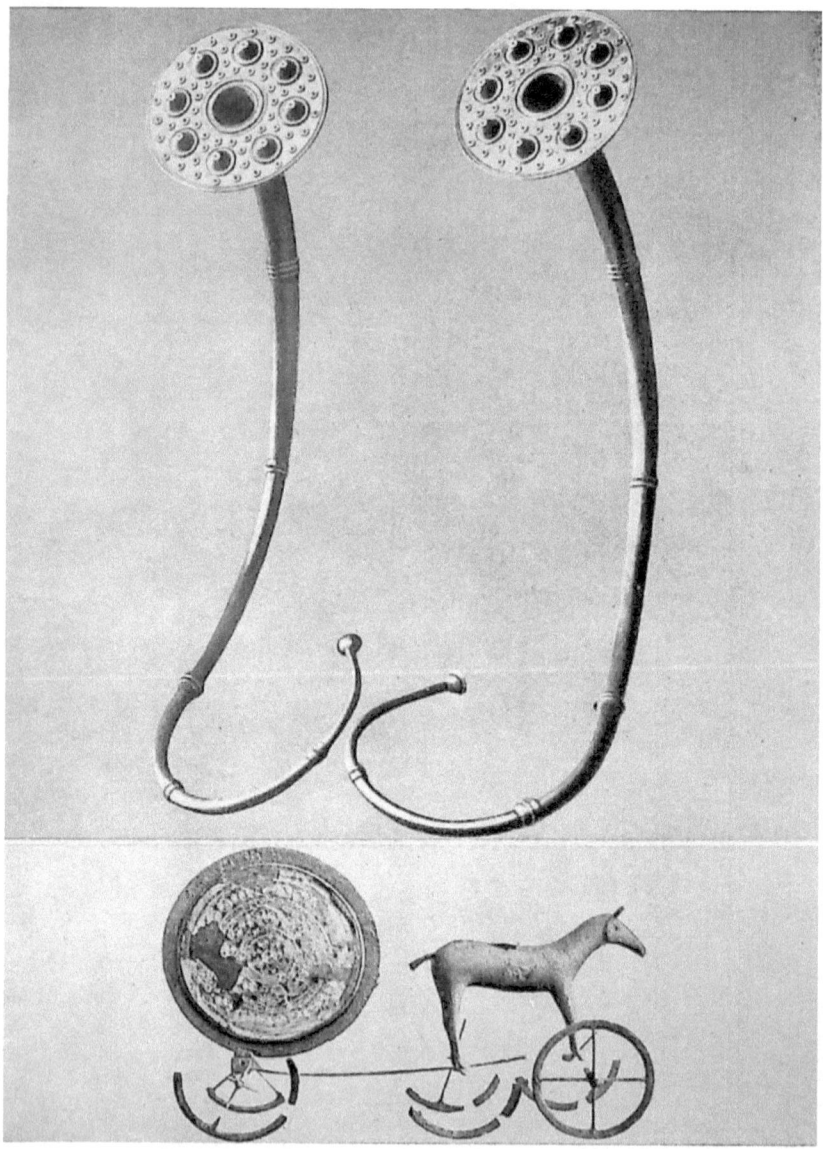

The lur and the sun chariot, two examples of highly advanced Germanic craftsmanship, are deeply rooted in Germanic traditions.

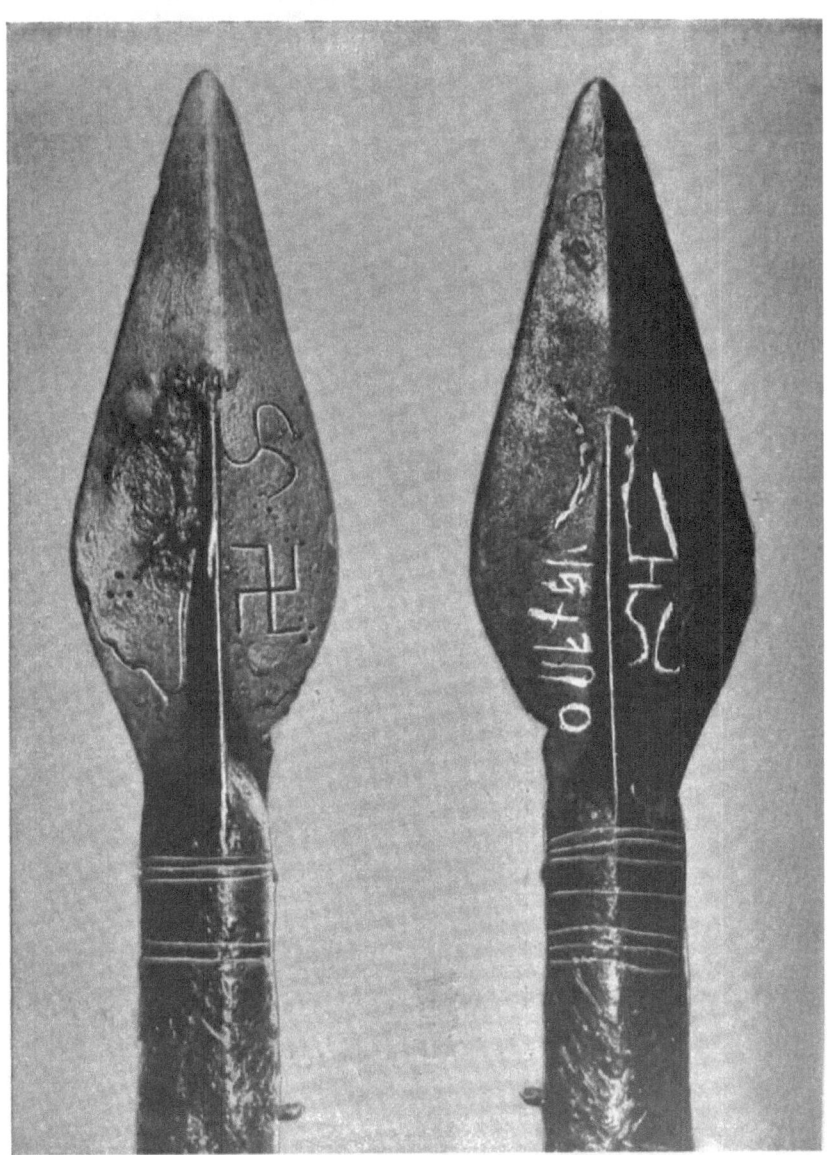

Iron Age spearheads with runic inscriptions and symbols

Helmet and swords, masterpieces of Germanic craftsmanship from the Iron Age

Clay vessels from the
Neolithic and Iron
Ages

Even everyday pottery was artfully
decorated.

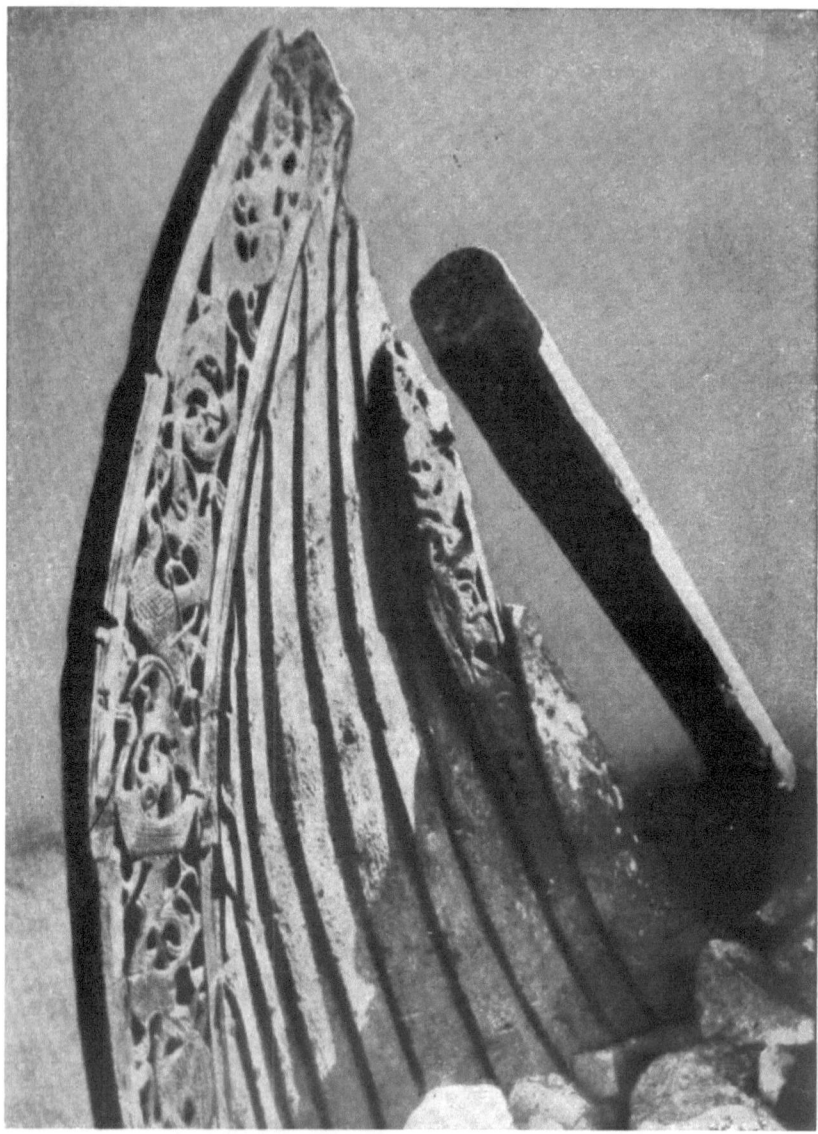

The elaborately decorated sternpost of the Oseberg ship…

...and the magnificently carved wagon from Oseberg, Norway, dating back to the Viking Age (ninth century ad)

chieftains could not protect the Hallstatt people when, around 500 BC, the Celts—originally led by a strong Nordic ruling class —invaded, likely from the Moselle region.[39] The Celts, in turn, were later displaced by the Germanic peoples.

Advance of the Germanic Peoples Into Southern Germany

Since the sixth century BC, individual Germanic tribes advanced from the region of the Lower Elbe to the Alps. In the first century BC, Southern Germany, including Alsace as far as Lake Constance, had not only been explored but also agriculturally settled by the Suebi coming from the Central Elbe region. The Suebi occupied the large refuge castles of the Celts in Southern

---

[39] The Moselle is a river in Northeastern France and Luxembourg, flowing toward Western Germany.

Germany;[40] moreover, large parts of what is now France were conquered by Ariovistus, king of the Suebi. The period of foreign domination by the Romans along the Rhine could not alter the distinct character of the Germanic peoples.

Onrush of the Germanic Peoples Across the Rhine

Julius Caesar, far-sighted as he was, knew that a Germanic Gaul would sooner or later spell the downfall of Rome. Only control of the Rhine could secure Roman dominance in Europe. After many fierce battles, Caesar managed to defeat the Germanic chieftain Ariovistus and push him back across the Rhine. Then, Caesar settled Germanic tribes on the left bank of the Rhine as a border guard against their kin in the east.

Arminius, the Guardian of Germanic Heritage

Caesar's successors continued this policy. However, to put an end to the incessant incursions of the Germanic tribes, Augustus decided to conquer inner Germania. Despite initial successes by the Romans, the actions of Arminius, the chieftain of the Cherusci, brought the Roman advance to an end at the Battle of the Teutoburg Forest in AD 9.

But Arminius' effort to unite the Germanic peoples in the struggle against Roman foreign rule was destroyed by betrayal. Although his plan was never fully realized, his endeavors gave the Nordic peoples and their culture time to develop and perfect themselves in their own unique way. Fate had decided against the uniform development of culture in Europe; apart from the Roman-dominated culture of the south, a Germanic-led culture of the north emerged. (See Map 5.)

---

[40] In Germanic history, a refuge castle was a fortification, usually atop of a hill, in which the population could take refuge in case of danger. They were not erected as residences for nobility.

Rome and Germania Respect One Another

Initially, relations with Rome were peaceful. The Battle of the Teutoburg Forest and the years of bitter combat that followed had led to a state of mutual respect, recognized by both sides. However, the strength of the Germanic peoples continued to develop thanks to their rapid population growth. Their accumulated strength would only surge over the confines of Roman power and culture—it was bound to happen.

Germanic Peoples During the Migration Period

And so it did. Historically, this period is known as the Migration Period. While entire tribes of East Germanic peoples were on the move, the West Germanic peoples pursued a systematic land-settlement policy from their established homelands. The individual tribes began to coalesce into larger confederations (the Frisii, Saxons, Thuringii, Franks, Alemanni, and Baiuvarii) as early as the fourth century AD, even before the introduction of Christianity. After numerous skirmishes on the border, they peacefully inhabited the Roman borderlands. The East Germanic peoples, however, left their East Prussian homelands and conquered ancient Rome.

Land and Migration Routes

The lack of land, brought about by Hunnic invasions, along with a thirst for action and a yearning for expansion and grandeur, drove the young warriors of the tribes in all directions. The Ostrogoths migrated from the Black Sea to Italy, the Visigoths from Transylvania to Spain, and the Vandals from Silesia and Northern Hungary to Africa. The Marcomanni migrated from Bohemia to Bavaria, and the Burgundians from the Baltic coast to the Upper Rhine and later to the Rhône River valley. The

Lombards migrated from the Lower Elbe to Italy, while the Suebi increasingly migrated to Southwestern Germany. (See Map 6.)

Obtrusion of the Slavic-Speaking Alpine Peoples Into the Germanic East

As a result, the Germanic eastern regions had become almost empty. Gradually, in the eighth and ninth centuries, Slavic-speaking Alpine peoples began to infiltrate the now sparsely populated Germanic eastern regions. It is regrettable that the majority of our ancestors left the Germanic east, leading to a permanent loss of precious German blood and soil. This land, lost to Slavic settlement, had to be reclaimed at great sacrifice through the German colonization of the east in the early Middle Ages. Nonetheless, we fully admire what the East Germanic peoples were able to accomplish in the south.

Foundation of the Germanic Kingdoms

Numerous kingdoms were now founded on Roman soil. (See Map 7.) These Germanic states along the Mediterranean, where the Germanic ruling class represented a permanent minority in relation to the subjugated Romans, were not sustainable. After a relatively short period of powerful growth, they were faced with ruin, because the people and their land were not united. Far from their homeland, in the midst of foreign cultures, the Germanic peoples ultimately abandoned their language, and with it, their racial consciousness. Wars waged against each other compounded their troubles, and above all, there were no reinforcements from the homeland. Thus, one after another, their kingdoms vanished, and their ethnic identity dissolved into foreign civilizations.

The immense racial influence the Germanic migrations had on the south is still evident today in the strong Nordic admixture in certain parts of France, Northern Italy, and the Balkans.

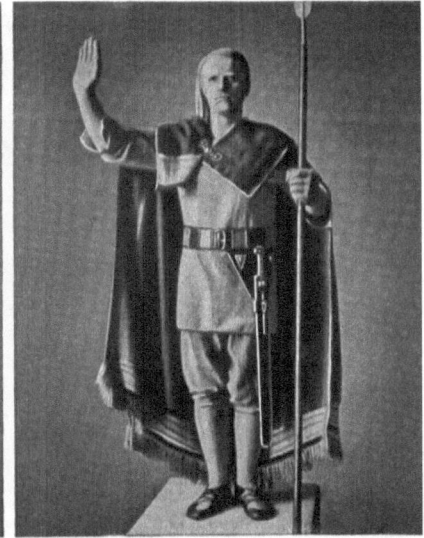

Exact reproductions of Germanic attire based on discoveries from the Iron Age

Germanic Capacity To Form States

We must rid ourselves of the mistaken notion that the Germanic peoples were inspired only by the fall of ancient Rome to form states of their own. Historians are increasingly realizing that the Germanic peoples were not only great lawgivers, but also great statesmen. The states of antiquity, namely Greece and Rome, were originally works of the Nordic peoples, as were the pre-medieval and medieval states of Europe.[41]

An example of this is the Germanic tribal states, of which the Kingdom of the Franks became the strongest, giving rise to the medieval German and French states. We also recognize the Nordic peoples as the original bearers and creators of other

---

[41] Some scholars (such as Karl Penka, Gustaf Kossinna and more recently, Jean Haudry) have suggested that certain states in the classical period, such as classical Greece or ancient Rome, were influenced by the migrations and cultural contributions of Nordic Indo-Europeans, thereby shaping the foundations of these civilizations. This theory is related to the North European hypothesis, which remains controversial today.

major European states: The English state is a creation of Anglo-Saxon and Norman peoples; the Spanish Empire arose from the Visigothic state; the state system of medieval Italy was influenced by Germanic peoples; the Russian state was founded by the Varangian chieftain Rurik; and the Scandinavian states were purely Germanic in origin.

Even before any contact with the massive Roman state, the Germanic peoples lived in racially conscious communities. Needless to say, the strong and high-minded sense of community led the Germanic peoples to a form of communal life that befitted their nature. Thus, even in early times, our Germanic ancestors were found to be part of well-organized and orderly communities of varying sizes.

Structure of Germanic Community

The nucleus of the Germanic state was the sib.[42] Above the sib was the village, then the *Gau,* and then the tribe.[43] Over a long period of time, these sibs merged into tribal communities. These tribal states were agrarian in nature. The full members of the tribe were the freemen who owned their land. These freemen—essentially the entire people—gathered in the tribal assembly. The tribal assembly was sovereign; it possessed legislative and judicial authority. It declared war and peace, and it dictated relations with other peoples. In times of war and conquest, it elected the king and entrusted him with executive authority.

---

[42] "Sib" is a technical term in anthropology that, in essence, refers to the group of people that an individual would recognize as his own kindred.

[43] The village was a collection of sibs, and the *Gau* was a cooperative of villages that shared communal resources such as pastures or woodlands. The tribe itself was a league of sibs across the various villages and *Gaue.*

Map 5: Germania during the Time of Arminius in the First Century AD

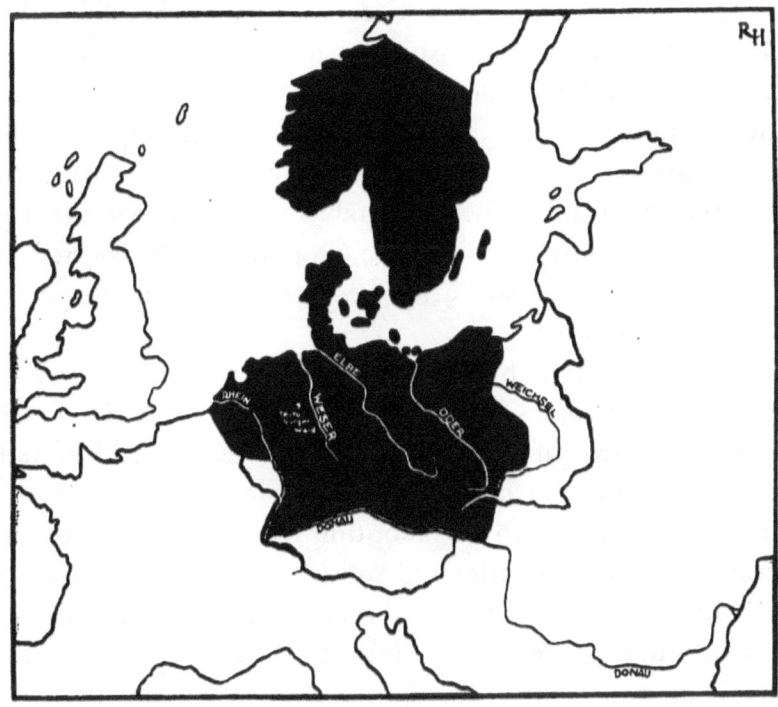

With his decisive action in the Teutoburg Forest, Arminius thwarted the Roman goal of extending the border of ancient Rome from the Rhine to the Elbe. Thus, Arminius the Liberator preserved the Germanic heartland, out of which the later German Reich would develop, from Romanization. This is his greatest historical contribution to Germany.

The borders of Germania during Arminius' time were approximately the Rhine, the Danube, and the Vistula rivers.

Emergence of Tribal Confederations

Around the third century, neighboring tribes, which were often distantly related, began to join together to form political confederations. Thus the tribal states of the Saxons, Thuringians, Bavarians, Swabians and Franks were established.

Advent of Christianity

In 325, Constantine the Great elevated the Christian doctrine of Bishop Athanasius—that Christ is God—to the exclusive official religion of the Roman Empire.[44] At that time, Rome's political power was steadily declining, and the Roman emperor sought to revitalize the state's vast structure with the help of a newly established organization: the Church. Over time, the Catholic Church adeptly asserted its spiritual and secular authority, becoming a dominant power throughout the world.

Rome had been shattered by the overwhelming force of the Germanic peoples during the Migration Period. However, as these waves of Germanic tribes penetrated Roman territories, they also began to racially mix with the native populations, leading to the adoption of Christianity. For the Germanic tribes that migrated southward, their resistance to this foreign teaching waned, because, through intermixing with southern races, they lost their impressive Nordic qualities.

In Germania itself, Christianization was systematically carried out by the Pope. Starting around 200, monks and bishops, under his directive, worked to blend Germanic concepts of God with Christian ideas, cleverly and deliberately embedding this foreign ideology into the Germanic peoples. The Germanic tribes largely adhered to the teachings of Arius, who asserted that Christ was only

---

[44] The First Council of Nicaea was convoked in 325 by Constantine the Great. Among other things, the council is notable for its strong condemnation of Arianism, which was an influential doctrine that denied the divinity of Christ. Despite being classified as a heresy, many Germanic peoples adhered to it in early medieval times. Bishop Athanasius of Alexandria was a very strong proponent of Christian orthodoxy against Arianism.

Map 6: The Migration Period of the Fourth Century

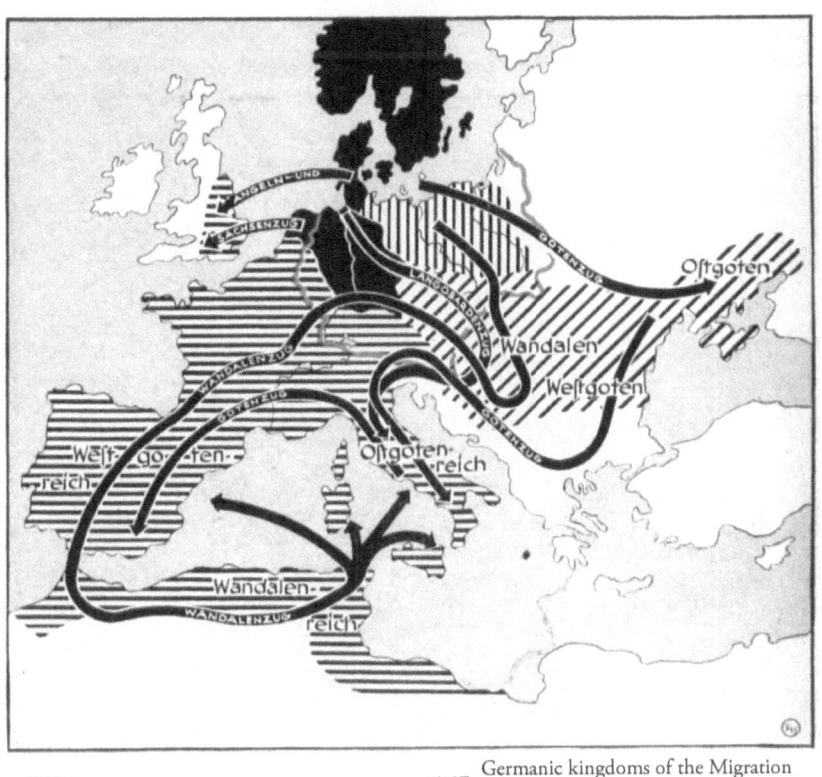

■ Unchanged Germanic lands	═══ Germanic kingdoms of the Migration Period
▥ Ancient Germanic lands (later partially vacated)	⁄⁄⁄ Germanic settlement areas (explored and later vacated)

In the fourth century, the migration of the Germanic peoples, which had begun long before, dramatically grew. The Goths in particular, and alongside them the Vandals, swept across Europe into its farthest corners. In the north, the Angles and Saxons conquered the land of the Celtic Britons.

The primary routes of the Migration Period were Goths via the Balkans and Italy to Spain, Vandals via the Balkans, France and Spain to North Africa, Lombards via Southern Germany to Northern Italy, and Angles and Saxons to Britain.

Map 7: Germanic Kingdoms in the Mediterranean around 500

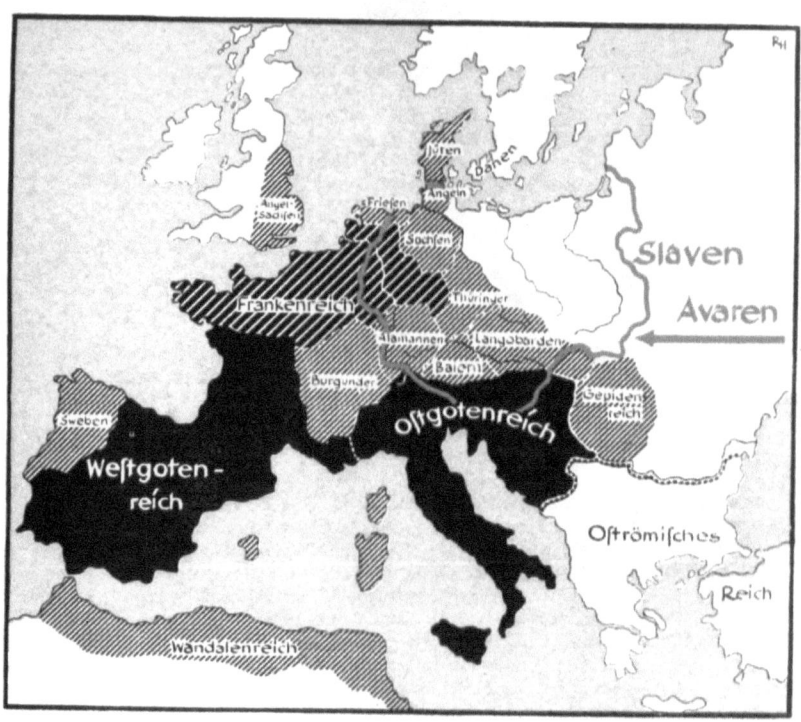

Around 500, the western Mediterranean was surrounded by vast Germanic kingdoms. In the far west, on the Iberian peninsula, the Visigoths, one of the most illustrious of all Germanic tribes, founded a new kingdom. The eastern Gothic tribe put an end to the aging Rome, where the Ostrogothic king Theodoric became ruler.

The Vandals, under their great king Gaiseric, crossed over to Africa and established a kingdom of seafaring warriors that dominated the Mediterranean. Such great and powerful Germanic kingdoms already existed in Europe and Africa at that time. The western Mediterranean had become a Germanic sea.

Despite that, these realms, established through conquest, eventually fell. They were kingdoms of noble warriors ruling over other peoples, and as the Germanic ruling class diluted their blood through intermarriage and expended it in wars, the kingdoms collapsed.

similar in essence to God.[45] Owing to their innate nature and disposition, the Germanic peoples could not accept the miraculous faith demanded by Athanasius. Nonetheless, they would eventually convert from this Arian creed to the Catholic faith.

This conversion obliterated every distinction that had been maintained between them and the mixed-race Roman population, even under Arianism. The Church—which at the most basic level refused to recognize racial differences—intentionally eliminated the distinctions between the Germanic peoples and the Roman subjects. Through miscegenation, these Germanic peoples lost their language and identity. Consequently, the noble Goths in Spain and Italy, the Vandals in Africa (those who were not entirely wiped out, that is), and the Lombards in Northern Italy were absorbed into the population of the Roman provinces. Although they infused the Romans with new cultural creativity with their blood, they themselves were severed from their own identity and thereby erased from history. By establishing monasteries and dioceses everywhere, the Pope created a power that would eventually become a curse upon the German people throughout their history.

---

[45] Arius, the Alexandrian presbyter after whom Arianism is named, taught that Christ was the Son of God but not truly divine; according to Arius, Christ was of a similar (although not the same) essence of God the Father.

CHAPTER THREE: THE FIRST REICH

Charlemagne: Founder of the State

Franks Develop a Structure for the State

Out of the chaos of the Migration Period, only one West Germanic tribe, the Franks, managed to structure their development into the form of a noteworthy state. The Franks migrated only a short distance and continuously received new strength from their homeland. Under Charles Martel, the Kingdom of the Franks, organized around the great cultural artery of the Rhine and its river system, still exhibited a distinctly Nordic attitude. He protected the Western world against the Moorish invasions with his victory at the Battle of Tours in 732. The donation of his son, Pepin the Short, which ratified papal possession of territories near Rome, Ravenna, and Ancona, laid the groundwork for the Papal States. This, in turn, substantiated the Pope's temporal claims and had the most disastrous consequences for the official German policy toward the Church.

Map 8: The Reich under Charlemagne

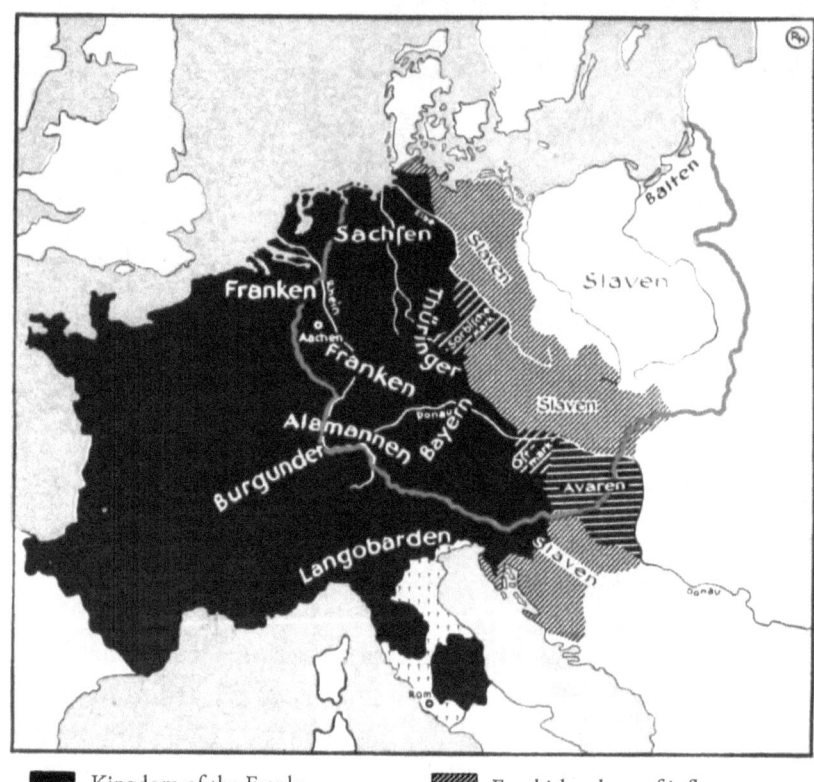

▰ Kingdom of the Franks	▨ Frankish sphere of influence
▰ Eastern marches	⦂ Papal States

From its Frankish heartland along the Middle and Lower Rhine, the Kingdom of the Franks under Charlemagne rose to a power that dominated Europe. Charlemagne's Reich encompassed present-day Germany up to the Elbe, present-day France, Spain up to the Ebro, Belgium, the Netherlands, Switzerland, and most of Italy.

Charlemagne established the eastern marches in front of his Reich, which became staging areas for future advances into the east.

With blood and sword, Charlemagne had built a Germanic-led Reich from the Germanic tribes, demonstrating its strength against the onslaught of Arab horsemen in the east and the Muslim Moors in the Pyrenees.

Height of the Kingdom of the Franks Under Charlemagne

The Kingdom of the Franks reached the height of its power under Charlemagne, the grandson of Charles Martel. He succeeded in uniting the Germanic tribes—the Bavarians, Saxons, Thuringians, and Alemanni—with the Franks, thereby creating a larger political entity. (See Map 8.) However, his Reich did not represent a union of people and territory. Essentially, he no longer ruled a purely Frankish realm, but a Franco-German Reich, a dual nature already reflected in the location of his royal residence in Aachen.

Charlemagne and Widukind

Nevertheless, Charlemagne intended for this Reich to have a distinctly Germanic character, and indeed, for the first time, he was the ruler of a vast, Germanic Reich. He also organized the initial bases for future eastward expansion.

Charlemagne, the great state builder

Henry the Fowler

Better dead than enslaved!

The indomitable spirit of the Saxons found its expression in their tragic struggle under Widukind

Charlemagne and Widukind

In pursuing his political ambitions, Charlemagne did not shy away from any means to unify the individual Germanic tribes. It was a harsh fate that the Saxon duke Widukind, who resisted Charlemagne the most, had to endure.[46] While we may reject Charlemagne's coercive methods today, we must acknowledge that he united the Europe of his time, making it into a powerful entity. Widukind, the defender of Germanic identity, and Charlemagne, the great state builder—they both exemplify the magnitude and influence of the Germanic peoples in history.

Foundations of the Carolingian Empire

The unified leadership and consolidated power contributed to many great achievements in the Carolingian Empire.[47] Owing to his exceptional personality, Charlemagne held the empire together and had the power to direct the Church according to his will. However, under his successors, the tensions between the divergent forces within the empire became increasingly apparent.

---

[46] Widukind was a Saxon leader and chief opponent of Charlemagne during the Saxon Wars. Though he eventually surrendered and was baptized into Christianity—formally ending major Saxon resistance—this conciliatory outcome followed years of brutal conflict. In 782, Charlemagne ordered the mass execution of 4,500 Saxons at Verden after they had surrendered, a stark example of the violence used to subjugate the region and enforce Christianization.

[47] During its history, the Frankish Empire (also known as the Kingdom of the Franks) was ruled by two dynasties: the Merovingian dynasty (fifth century to 751) and the Carolingian dynasty. Thus, the term "Carolingian Empire" refers to the Frankish Empire under the rule of the Carolingian dynasty, which came to political power with Charlemagne.

Louis' Dependence on Rome

In place of a church subordinate to the state, there emerged a politically powerful church based in Rome, and Charlemagne's son, Louis the Pious, became the compliant tool of this new power. Over time, the Roman parts of the Frankish Empire grew increasingly isolated from the Germanic regions. Incompetent heirs on the imperial throne further exacerbated the situation, leading to the division of the empire in the Treaty of Verdun in 843 and again with the Treaty of Meerssen in 870.[48]

---

[48] There were four partition treaties of the Carolingian Empire, including the Treaties of Verdun and Meerssen. The Treaties of Prüm (855) and Ribemont (880) were the other two. They were agreements that divided the Frankish Empire among Charlemagne's grandsons, leading to the formation of distinct territories that laid the foundations for modern European states.

CHAPTER FOUR: THE REICH IN THE MIDDLE AGES

Henry the Fowler: Founder of the First German Reich

Partition of the Frankish Empire

The forced unity of Germany and France shattered under the sons of Louis the Pious into three parts. The easternmost part—the ancient Germanic heartland, modern Germany—comprised the Germanic tribes of the East Franks, Saxons, Swabians, Bavarians, and Lotharingians. Even after this partition, East Francia's cohesion continued to unravel; the individual tribes regained their strength as royal power grew weaker and powerful dukes emerged. The first ruler to unite the splintering tribes and lay the foundations for the first truly German Reich was Henry the Fowler, the Duke of Saxony.

German Reich

With that, the leadership of the kingdom passed to the German tribe that had preserved the purest form of its Germanic character, where landowning peasants represented the majority of its population.

The first Saxon king, Henry the Fowler, restored unity using shrewd policies regarding the tribes. He consciously avoided too close a tie with the Church. By doing so, the political influence of the Catholic Church was driven back, laying the foundation for the true unity of a German Reich. (See Map 9.)

Power in the King's Hands

Once he succeeded in gaining control over the entire land, the power that the German king wielded was immense for that time. There was no realm that could compete with the German state. In the west, the French monarchy was sinking into impotence, and in the south, Italy was still fragmented, owing to the disintegration of the Frankish Empire. In modern terms, Germany was the only great power in the Western world.

History and Geopolitics

What tasks did this great power now complete? In general, each state is assigned its tasks externally, that is, by the location and nature of the land. The geography of a land dictates to every state how it must defend itself and how it can and should grow. Therefore, the constant factor that most strongly influences the political history of all times is geography. Today, we refer to this perspective as geopolitics.

German history, from the very beginning, has been under the influence of its geographical position. This geography presents a problem that has persisted through the centuries to the present day and is now visible even to the untrained eye: the problem of a double front.

War on two fronts is, in a sense, the leitmotif of German history. This of course stems from the fact that Germany is a landlocked country, situated between large and diverse neighboring nations, only separated from them by weak or non-existent natural boundaries. This became apparent even during the formation of the early German state, manifesting in simultaneous conflicts in both the east and the west.

Western Border

In the west, the German realm initially had a seemingly perfect border, reaching up to the Rhine and the Vosges Mountains. The territories beyond the left bank of the Rhine, the former Kingdom of Lotharingia—in today's terms, Lorraine, the Rhenish Palatinate, the Rhineland, the Netherlands, and Belgium up to the Scheldt River—had not seceded from the Carolingian Empire and had thus become "French." Had it remained that way, Germany would have gained a natural border at the cost of losing other territories, resulting in a permanent mutilation. This loss was not only of a significant portion of the German population but also of lands that were among the most populated, wealthy, and civilized north of the Alps, far ahead of the rest of Germany. It is important to remember that much of what the German realm encompassed at that time was still culturally underdeveloped.

Henry the Fowler Acquires Lotharingia

For these reasons, relinquishing Lotharingia would have meant suicide for the German realm, relegating it to insignificance. Henry the Fowler wisely seized the opportunity to gain recognition as ruler over Lotharingia for himself, thereby winning this valuable territory for Germany.

Mission in the East

The mission in the east was not so simple. Only after fierce battles were the Hungarians, formidable opponents that they were, pushed back beyond the Leitha River in Lower Austria. Following the victorious campaigns, a stream of German settlers from

Bavaria and Southern Ostmark began to flow in, beginning the permanent Germanization of Ostmark.[49]

Dealing with the other Slavic-speaking neighbors in the east was easier, particularly with the Wends beyond the Elbe, the Saale, and the Bohemian Forest. They were neither militarily dangerous nor politically unified, being a collection of small tribes with little strength in times of war or peace. The land between the Saale and Elbe was secured, as was the annexation of Bohemia, which Bismarck once called the "citadel of Europe" owing to its strategic location. This fortress became valuable when, around the year 1000, a unified Polish kingdom emerged and began to expand at the expense of the German territories, only to disintegrate soon after.

Two ardent German noblemen in particular strengthened and expanded German colonization efforts in the east in the tenth century: Hermann Billung, who was entrusted with the Duchy of Saxony in 961, and Gero, who extended the German territory to the Oder River and even defeated the Polish duke Mieszko I.

Thus, the obvious missions in both the west and east were accomplished, and Germany's borders were secured through the weakness of its neighbors. The German people appeared to have the choice to expand either to the east, to the west, or simultaneously in both directions.

They did neither. They were content to keep their neighbors in check without even thinking of conquering Poland; thus, colonization efforts stopped at the borders of what was actually Magyar territory in the south, and there was certainly no talk of expanding westward.

---

[49] Ostmark, originally a border march of the Carolingian Empire in the early Middle Ages, corresponds to the modern region of Austria and played a crucial role in defending the eastern frontier of the empire.

Call of the South

Instead, since the middle of the tenth century, attention was continuously directed to the south. Italy became the focus of German foreign policy, German settlement, and the expansion of German power.

Emergence of the German Empire

We thus enter a new epoch: the emergence of the German empire.[50] It dominates the entirety of early German history, spanning three centuries. Even later, when it had long ceased to exist in reality, its memory continued to exert a powerful and still-growing influence.

The Increase in Power of Ecclesiastical and Secular Princes

Increase in the Church's Power Under Otto the Great

Otto the Great, the son of Henry, made the first attempt to subjugate Northern Italy and had himself crowned emperor in Rome. Under Otto, the power of the Church increased once again. In Italy, as in Germany itself, the Church became the mainstay of the imperial government. Only the emperor could grant the bishops their imperial immediacy.[51] With that came their political power against the western dynasties that sought to

---

[50] The language used here may be somewhat confusing in English. The author is referring to the "First Reich," known today as the Holy Roman Empire, ruled by a series of German monarchs following the resurrection of the imperial title by Emperor Otto I.

[51] Immediacy refers to the status of landed nobility who are subject only to the emperor, and not to any other liege lord. Immediate imperial vassals, known as Imperial Princes or Fürsten, held a great deal of political power and autonomy within the Empire.

subjugate the bishops in Italy. The matter proved more difficult in Rome. However, the idea eventually took hold that the German emperor, just as he was king of Italy, was also emperor of the Romans. Germany, Italy, and Rome (that is, the Church) united, and the elected king of Germany was simultaneously ruler of the entire empire, which came to be known as the Holy Roman Empire.[52]

Relationship of the Bishops With the Emperor and the Pope

Bishops, these high-ranking ecclesiastical dignitaries on whom the empire relied, were under the authority of the Pope. This was not a problem so long as imperial power remained strong in Germany and the papacy remained powerless. However, when the balance of power shifted, the imperial authority—only ever recognized and accepted by the western power brokers with reluctance—became a pawn of the ecclesiastical rulers. These clerics wielded two heavy weapons in any emerging dispute. Firstly, the vast ecclesiastical landholdings, which remained property of the Church, were inviolable regardless of the diocesan administrator in charge. If the king removed a troublesome administrator from office, the next one would simply take over, and the cycle would start anew. Secondly—and most decisively—the clergy held the conscience of the common people in the palm of their hands through consistent and continuous pastoral care. Given the inherently pious nature of the German people, this represented an extremely powerful tool, capable of undermining even the most popular monarchy.

The day the Church renounced obedience to the king, and the Pope became the emperor's enemy, the very foundations of

---

[52] During the time of Otto the Great, the constituent kingdoms of the Holy Roman Empire were Germany and Italy, each with its own distinct territory and governance but unified under the rule of the emperor. The list of constituent kingdoms would grow to include Burgundy and eventually Bohemia.

Map 9: The Reich under Henry the Fowler in 936

■	Germanic tribes in the Reich	←	Hungarian attacks
▨	Eastern marches	◄·····	
		━	Eastern border

The multi-ethnic empire of Charlemagne (with Romans in the west and Germanic peoples in the east) fragmented under his inept heirs. It was Henry the Fowler who succeeded in powerfully uniting the splintered Germanic tribes of the Frisians, Saxons, Franks, Swabians, and Bavarians under his leadership, thus building a purely Germanic empire. The old Rhenish-Franconian heartland, Lotharingia, was incorporated into the empire in 925; since then, the Rhineland has been an inseparable part of Germany.

Henry vigorously pursued the eastward expansion begun by Charlemagne, advancing as far as the Oder. He also brought Bohemia under his control in 928. His successor, Otto the Great, extended the frontier further southeast to Styria and Carinthia. With this unified strength, Germany could successfully repel the recurring invasions from the Asiatic east. The Hungarians were decisively defeated at the Battle of Riade in 933 under Henry and at the Battle of Lechfeld in 955 under Otto.

the state and the empire, as well as the monarchy itself, would be thrown into doubt.

The Clash Between the Emperor and the Pope

That day came. The empire and the Church split in the 1070s and clashed bitterly with each other for nearly fifty years. When the conflict finally ended, it was not true peace that was achieved but merely a truce. The empire and the Church remained adversaries, often seeking a lasting reconciliation but never truly finding it. The ultimate result was the downfall of the German monarchy and the dissolution of the German state.

Dominion of the Church Over the World

Under the protection of the empire, Rome had grown ever more powerful. Pope Gregory VII, in his arrogance, even rejected the investiture of bishops and abbots by secular princes. Such a challenge was aimed directly against imperial authority and was effectively a death blow to the well-being of the empire. The German crown had to fight against this new measure with all its might, as its very existence was at stake.[53]

In addition to his ideas for ecclesiastical reform, Gregory introduced a new concept: the authority of the Church over the world.[54] In a literal sense, the Prince of the Apostles was to hold

---

[53] In 1075, Pope Gregory VII affirmed *Dictatus papae* ("The Dictation of the Pope"), in which he withdrew the power of secular rulers to appoint bishops, thus initiating the prolonged conflict between the Pope and the emperor known as the Investiture Controversy.

[54] Gregory was the most vocal advocate of a series of reforms aimed at rooting out corruption in the Catholic Church; hence, it is known as the Gregorian reform. These changes included enforcing clerical celibacy and ending the practice of simony and lay investiture.

sway over earth as well as heaven.[55] He could decide and rule over all earthly matters, giving and taking according to merit. All kings and princes were obliged to obey him, as they were rightfully his vassals and liegemen.

When the Pope demanded that the emperor comply with these almost unbelievable demands, open conflict ensued.

Henry IV Versus Gregory VII

Henry IV continued to appoint bishops at his discretion. When threatened with ecclesiastical penalties, the emperor responded by declaring the Pope deposed. In turn, Gregory VII excommunicated him, casting him out of the Christian community and releasing his subjects from their oaths of allegiance to him as emperor.

It soon became clear who was stronger. The German nobles seized the opportunity to overthrow their king, who had become too powerful, and they allied with the Pope. The bishops, who were both secular leaders—dependent on the emperor—and spiritual leaders, lacked the courage to openly fight against the Pope, their ecclesiastical head. Was the empire now on the brink of collapse? To break his opposition and save the empire, Henry decided to submit to the Church.

Canossa

Through an act of personal penance at the gates of Canossa in late January 1077, where he had intercepted the Pope on his way to Germany, Henry persuaded Gregory to lift the excommunication. Henry was thus able to rule again, but the reputation of Germany, the dignity of the German king, and the concept of the emperor had

---

[55] The title "Prince of the Apostles" refers to the Pope. Saint Peter was the first "Prince of the Apostles," because he was regarded as the foremost among Jesus' twelve apostles, and his authority is passed down through apostolic succession to each subsequent Pope.

suffered immense damage.

But that was not the end of it. The conflict raged on unabated. The Pope skillfully exploited the rift between the emperor and his princes to drive German power out of Italy and establish himself as the head of the Italian states. Rome had reluctantly accepted the emperor's power, but reserved its future ambitions. The papacy remained the old adversary and principal opponent of the empire. The result of this conflict marked the end of the emperorship, signifying the end of German dominance in the west and the beginning of the dissolution of the empire.

Fatal Error of the German Princes

The failure of the empire can be attributed to more than just the clash between the emperor and the Pope. It also fell apart as a result of the disunity, selfishness and short-sightedness of the German princes. Who can overlook the fact that certain detrimental traits, which appear repeatedly throughout German history, had such fatal consequences?

The lack of a sense of unity and common purpose, the preference for individual interests over collective ones and the weakness of political instinct—these national shortcomings are why Germany missed its opportunity to maintain a dominant position in the Western world at the turn of the twelfth century.

Imperial Crown Grows Weaker

As external successes faded and the empire's power collapsed, the internal state of the Reich became clear. The king no longer had control of the princes, because he had lost much of his former authority. Meanwhile, the power of the princes had grown. They now ruled over unified territories that continued to expand, while the royal estates crumbled away. The crown was weakened, and its rivals had become stronger.

The princes were no longer the tribal dukes of old. The ancient duchies existed in name only and had diminished in size from partitions. In 976, Carinthia had separated from the Duchy of Bavaria to become an independent duchy. Austria followed in 1156, and Styria in 1180. Saxony was divided in 1180 between Cologne and Anhalt. Swabia managed to remain intact for a while, but after the Hohenstaufen dynasty ended, it too was divided among its neighbors.[56]

Local States Rise to Power

We observe widespread fragmentation and disintegration. Instead of consolidating into large power structures, peoples developed toward division and splintering. However, this did not weaken the principalities; it actually strengthened them. The smaller territories were easier to govern and allowed for stronger cohesion. What the principalities lost in size, they gained in stability.

In the second half of the twelfth century, actual local governments and states emerged. The empire, and the rule of the king, was essentially just a collection of overlordships. Real governing power—courts, police, armed protection, customs, minting, and above all, the right to levy taxes—lay in the hands of the local lords. The king was limited to overlordship, which he exercised only occasionally.

Why the Empire Was Defeated

The episcopate was never meant to provide stability to the empire. As clergy, they were obligated to obey the Pope. As princes of the empire, they became independent local rulers, just like the dukes before them, each one a ruler of his own state with its own

---

[56] The Hohenstaufen dynasty was a powerful medieval royal family that ruled the Holy Roman Empire for over a century; members of the house played significant roles in European politics and the Crusades.

responsibilities and interests. The affairs of the empire concerned them little, for they had nothing to expect of the crown except perhaps the fear that their newly granted rights might be curtailed.

These factors played out in Germany just as the empire was declining in Italy.

Today, we believe that this decline could have been avoided if the German kings had first strengthened their power at home before taking on major foreign endeavors. It was unnatural for the focus of German power to lie outside of Germany. The kings, focused on Rome, overlooked the more urgent tasks in Germany itself. They failed to see the Slavic tide from the east threatening the empire's borders, encroaching on originally German lands year after year. The loyalty of the local princes could only be ensured if the emperor decided to prioritize his role as German king over the title of ruler of the Holy Roman Empire of the German Nation.

The most decisive reason for the clash between the empire and the papacy was the question of supreme authority. Who holds the highest power in the Western world to which the people owe their deepest allegiance? Is it the state, emperor, and king, or is it the church, Pope, and cleric? It was a battle for the soul of the nation. So why did the emperor lose the struggle?

The structure of the Church was stronger than that of the state. The Pope united his clergy into a cohesive unit and trained them to be entirely under papal authority and loyal to himself. With this organization, he triumphed. The emperor lacked this strong organization. The feudal system of dukes and counts was not nearly stable enough. Additionally, the geographical distance between Germany and Italy posed a problem. Military campaigns lasted for years, causing the leaders to become alienated from their people.

The Crusades: Rome's New Show of Force

The rise of the Church's political power throughout the entire civilized world found new expression in the Crusades. Today, it may strike us as odd that the peoples of Europe were spontaneously captivated by an idea that championed the liberation of the Holy Sepulcher from Islamic rule.[57] However, we also know what a momentous power any idea can have if the will of its standard bearer is unwavering.

The driving force behind the Crusades was the Catholic Church. It was a new show of force from the political papacy, which sought to establish itself as the supreme leader of the West. For the German people, these campaigns led to another weakening of their Nordic blood, resulting in the loss of many of their best men for a senseless war. This would be a decisive turning point in German history.

The Hohenstaufen dynasty gave the empire one of the greatest representatives of German imperial glory in Frederick Barbarossa.[58] During his reign, Henry the Lion resumed the fight for the German east.[59] Then, as the empire's power continued to decline throughout the thirteenth century, the German people—through their burghers, peasants, and the Teutonic Order—achieved one of their most brilliant feats by colonizing the east.[60]

Functional End of the Empire

While the Crusades were taking place under the rule of the

---

[57] The Holy Sepulcher is another term for the tomb of Jesus, which at that time was under the control of the Islamic caliphate.

[58] Frederick Barbarossa, widely considered one of the greatest Holy Roman Emperors, was a renowned German ruler known for his extraordinary leadership, successful military campaigns and shrewd efforts to consolidate imperial power, leaving a lasting legacy in both German and European history.

[59] Henry the Lion was a powerful German duke known for his role in reconquering and expanding German territories in Central and Eastern Europe, significantly influencing the region's development and settlement.

[60] The Teutonic Order was a medieval Catholic military order that played a significant role in the German eastward expansion by promoting the settlement and Christianization of Eastern Europe, particularly in Prussia and the Baltic regions.

Hohenstaufen dynasty, the Holy Roman Empire also effectively ceased to exist. (See Map 10.) Although it retained its name and the title of emperor remained, the fundamental principles that gave those words any significance had been totally altered. Up to that point, the empire had retained a predominantly German character in both its ruling houses and its internal power structure, but this now entirely shifted.

Habsburgs Shift the Empire's Focus to the South

Under the subsequent leadership of the House of Habsburg, the Holy Roman Empire shifted its focus to the territories more closely aligned with the Roman papacy.[61] The German nation, which had previously been the main power of the empire, was more or less politically sidelined. As a result, it gradually fell into a state of internal disintegration, evident in its petty conflicts, feuds among nobility and cities warring with one another.

Guild System

It is remarkable, and often seems paradoxical, that a people who struggled so much to form a cohesive empire could nevertheless create such powerful and robust organizations like the guild system.[62]

City Governance

Similarly, the governance of the cities, which can be seen as a

---

[61] The House of Habsburg was a prominent European dynastic family that rose to power in the late Middle Ages, becoming one of the most influential royal houses, and would rule over the Holy Roman Empire for centuries.

[62] The guild system in the Middle Ages was an organization of artisans and merchants that regulated trade, maintained quality standards, protected the economic interests of its members within a particular craft or industry. It also provided social and economic benefits such as training, support and communal protection, thereby contributing to the economic stability and development of many European cities.

further development of the guilds, was so strong that the golden age of the Hohenstaufen reign was more rooted in these aspects than in any imperial policy. It was the people themselves who rose up and thrived, despite the constant drain on resources caused by the emperors and their campaigns in Italy.[63]

Settling Eastern Germany: the Teutonic Order and the Hanseatic League

Two organizations in particular, which would go on to become pre-eminent in Germany, arose organically from the people. As such, they demonstrate both the strength of the German people and the failings of the emperors over the centuries. These organizations are the Teutonic Order and the Hanseatic League. Both bore the German spirit at a time when the great nobility of this fractured Empire squabbled over the imperial throne. Later, when the House of Habsburg finally assumed power, these organizations were crucial, as the Habsburgs exposed their indifference to Germany by focusing solely on consolidating their own power.

Teutonic Order

This laid the foundation for a new eastward colonization. (See Map 11.) And it was the Teutonic Order that ventured east, bringing the Vistula region—an ancient Germanic land—back into German civilization. The conquests of the Order's knights

---

[63] The guild system and local governance of medieval Germany contributed to the golden age of the Hohenstaufen dynasty by fostering economic growth, stability and urban development. The guilds ensured high standards of craftsmanship and facilitated trade, which increased wealth and economic power in the cities. Meanwhile, a structured form of self-governance allowed cities to flourish as centers of commerce and culture, enhancing the overall prosperity of the Reich. This economic and political strength supported the Hohenstaufens' ambitions, enabling them to pursue expansive policies in Europe.

spread German culture deep into the Baltic region. For seven centuries, the land and its rich cultural heritage remained predominantly German, even though the Order began to crumble from within by 1410, leading to its eventual dissolution.[64] It was only in 1918 that Latvian Bolshevism, with the tacit approval of the Entente, managed to decimate German culture in the Baltics.[65] This was only possible because the Order had failed to thoroughly colonize the Baltic farmers and craftsmen, as they had done in Prussia itself. There was an already settled population of Germans in Prussia. However, in the Baltics, the knights stood alone, without the backing of a large German population.

Like a warning of fate, the words "blood and soil" stand before us once again, symbolizing the mysterious wellspring of our ethnic life.[66]

This is also the essential difference between the Teutonic Order and the *Schutzstaffel*. The Teutonic Order was a league of men, whereas the *Schutzstaffel* represents a true brotherhood within the national community. The celibacy of the knights was a tragic portent of their impending decline in a land ruled by others. Ultimately, only a state built organically on a healthy and large population has the right to exist.

---

[64] In 1410, the Battle of Grunwald was a major conflict in which the Polish-Lithuanian union decisively defeated the Teutonic Order, marking the beginning of the Order's decline as a major military and political power in Eastern Europe.

[65] In 1918, after a Bolshevik government seized control, a wave of Red Terror swept through the rural and urban regions of Latvia. The widespread destruction of German culture in the Baltics began with the Bolshevik revolutionaries targeting German institutions and landowners, while the Entente powers, concerned with containing both German and Bolshevik influence, supported local nationalist forces, which only contributed to the decline of Baltic German influence in the region.

[66] The concept of "blood and soil" emphasized the idea that the German people ("blood") were intrinsically linked to their native homeland ("soil"), giving grounds for irredentist foreign policy aimed at acquiring more territory to support and sustain the German nation. This sentence here appears to be an exhortation to the reader (originally soldiers in the SS) to bear in mind the significance of the Eastern Front to the long-term success of the Third Reich.

Map 10: The Reich during the Hohenstaufen Era in the First Half of the Thirteenth Century

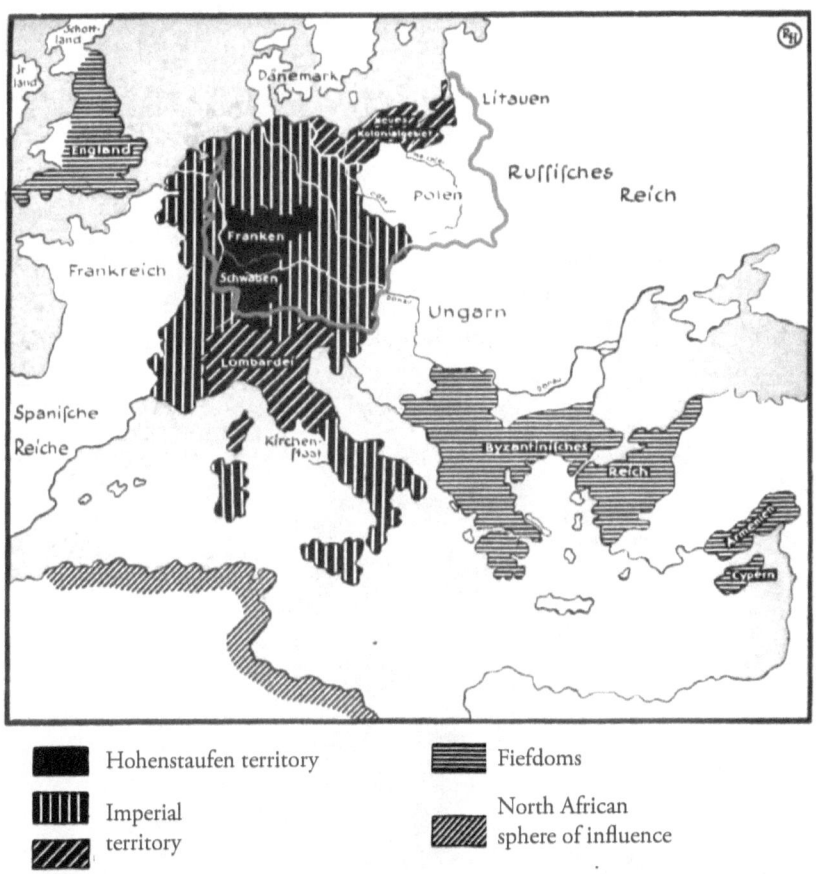

	Hohenstaufen territory		Fiefdoms
	Imperial territory		North African sphere of influence

The empire began its massive expansion under Otto the Great and reached its peak under the Hohenstaufens. However, it eventually fell apart under their leadership, as its growth had become unmanageable.

For three hundred years, until the mid-thirteenth century, the empire was the leading power in Europe. It expanded massively in two directions: east and south. The emperors' campaigns to the south were necessary to prevent the politically ambitious papacy from establishing Italy as a power base to dominate the empire. These southern campaigns brought the empire prestige and power but also made it vulnerable, as the extent of the empire became too vast for any ruler to manage effectively.

At its peak, the Hohenstaufens' empire included Germany up to the Oder River, Switzerland, Italy, and a large part of France. Even North Africa, parts of the eastern Mediterranean, and Britain to the north were under the influence of the emperor.

The Duchy of Prussia, originally a territory of the Order, eventually came under the control of the Elector of Brandenburg about two hundred fifty years later, thanks to its last Grand Master, Albert of Brandenburg.[67]

Hanseatic League

The second most significant development of this era was the rise of the prosperous Hanseatic League. It provided the political and economic support for German influence in the newly acquired territories of the Teutonic Order. The Hanseatic League evolved from an association of

Hanseatic ship

---

[67] The Prussian Homage in 1525 marked the end of the Teutonic Order's control over Prussia, which became a Protestant duchy under foreign suzerainty, signaling a significant decline in the Order's already weakened political power and influence. This coincided with Albert of Brandenburg's conversion to Protestantism. All this paved the way for the eventual establishment of the powerful Kingdom of Prussia in 1701, which would last until the end of the First World War.

German merchants, particularly in the Baltic Sea, into a confederation of German cities stretching from Reval in the northeast to Bruges in the northwest. Lübeck, the "Queen of the Hanseatic League," replaced the original center of Visby on Gotland.[68] Hanseatic trading posts were established in Novgorod, Bergen, and London.

It was during this time that coinage began to be used as a medium of exchange in trade throughout Germany. However, every small prince and town minted its own coin, which at that time made trade and monetary transactions quite challenging. The actual value of the coins depended almost entirely on the wealth and stability of the issuing city.

Golden Age of the Hanseatic League

By 1350, the Hanseatic League emerged as a political power with a large and well-equipped navy, controlling both the North Sea and the Baltic Sea. Owing to their economic dominance, the Hanseatic cities received monopolistic trading privileges from foreign rulers. Even King Valdemar IV of Denmark had to yield to the united political power of the Hanseatic cities. At that time, the Hanseatic League reached its peak under the leadership of Hamburg.

Decline of the Hanseatic League

The formation of the Kalmar Union in 1397, which united the three Nordic kingdoms, presented the Hanseatic League with a united front that put a halt to its expansion—and thus to the spread of German influence in the north. The Hanseatic League lacked leaders who might have forged new paths for expanding its power. Consequently, this period of stagnation led to the

---

[68] Reval today is known as Tallinn, the capital of Estonia, and Bruges is a city in Northern Belgium. Lübeck is a port city in Northern Germany, and Visby is a city on the Swedish island of Gotland.

inevitable decline of the Hanseatic League's influence.

Conquests of Other Nations in the World

During the Age of Discovery, the Portuguese, Spanish, Dutch, and later the English led their nations into the world. As these

German Crusaders and knights of the Teutonic Order

In addition to a helmet and shield, the chainmail hauberk also protected the body of German Crusaders (left). A German knight of the Teutonic Order (right).

countries expanded their trade across the ocean and brought the riches and goods of exotic lands to Europe, the Hanseatic League, already in decline, lacked the leadership to recognize the significance of these developments.

At that moment, the fate of the Hanseatic League was sealed. It had dwindled into a minor inland shipping company, losing the foundation of its power and, consequently, its political strength.

Historical Significance of the Teutonic Order and the Hanseatic League

The Teutonic Order and the Hanseatic League provided essential support for German colonization and influence in the neighboring countries to the east and north. The empire had no hand in their formation and never supported them later. The saddest part of the drama that is medieval German colonialism is that it was driven entirely by local powers, without the support of a strong central authority, yet it was still deeply imbued with a conscious national spirit. The Teutonic Order was truly German, as was the Hanseatic League.

Just as the Hanseatic League knew no other purpose than to defend common German interests abroad, the Teutonic Order was fundamentally closed to anything not of German origin, making it the only strictly national religious order of the Middle Ages. The driving forces behind such an expansive, unified, and conscious movement, arising spontaneously from the local needs of the time without any centralized plan or directive, must have been incredibly strong. While one cannot help but be amazed at this sight, it also evokes a sense of regret. One can only imagine what could have been achieved with such forces under the unified and strategic leadership of a strong central authority.

However, such an authority was entirely lacking, and so the results were ultimately unsatisfactory everywhere. The necessary

Map 11: Eastward Expansion from the Twelfth Century

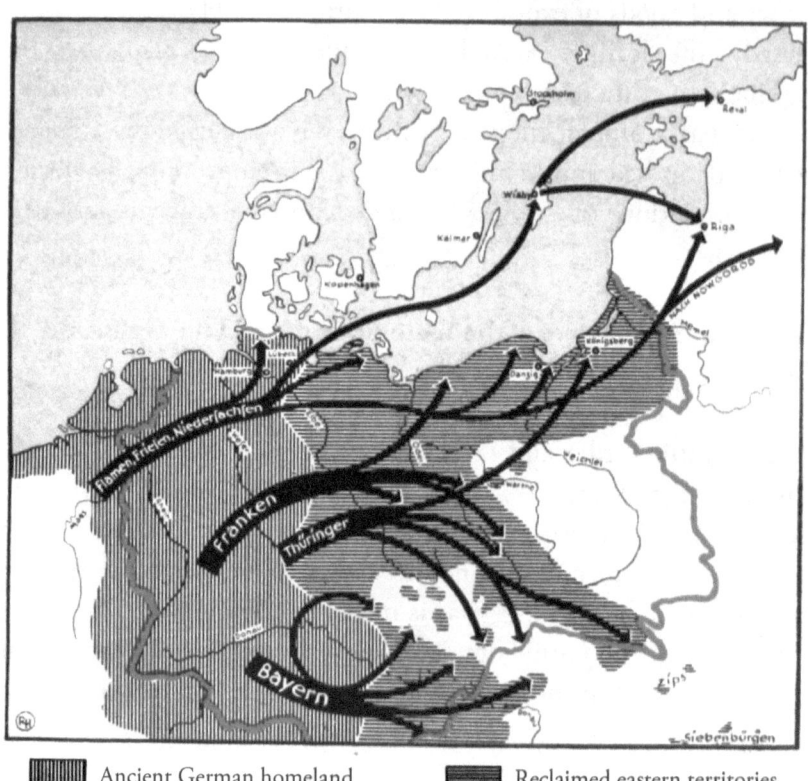

▥ Ancient German homeland	▦ Reclaimed eastern territories

From the twelfth century onward, the repopulation of the east was a collective effort by all the Germanic tribes. The earliest settlers in the south were Bavarian peasants; they moved beyond the old border at the Enns River into the Great Hungarian Plain, crossing the mountains of Carinthia and Tyrol into the Italian and formerly South Slavic lands.

Starting from Upper Franconia and the former Sudetenland, the settlement expanded to include the interior lowlands of Bohemia. The reclamation of the east was achieved with especially methodical vigor from Central and Northern Germany. Notable figures in this effort included Henry the Lion, Albert the Bear, and the Teutonic Knights.

German settlements sprang up all over the east—in the Baltics, inner Poland, Bohemia, Hungary, and even in regions like Spiš and Transylvania.

Map 12: The State of the Teutonic Order in the Thirteenth and Fourteenth Centuries

|||||||| State of the Teutonic Order

The Teutonic Order, through arduous and diligent effort, established a state stretching from the Vistula River valley across the entire Baltic region. Until its tragic downfall at the Battle of Grunwald in 1410, this state stood as a strong bulwark against the eastern hordes.

conclusions were never reached, leading to the border taking on an impractical shape. For instance, trade between Livonia and Prussia was primarily established via the sea, because the conquest of Samogitia, which lies between the two, was neglected.[69]

The German colonization of the east is the greatest achievement of the German people in the Middle Ages, a feat that alone would secure their place among the leading civilizations of the world.

One need only look at the vast area on the map. (See Map 12.) It had been a wilderness that was transformed by the Germans into a land of great culture. This achievement can be compared to what the Romans accomplished with their conquered provinces in ancient times.

German Settlers Are Called To Foreign Lands

The effects of German colonization extended far beyond the borders of the newly acquired territories of the empire. They had reached across all of Poland and Galicia, stretching as far as the Ukraine and Romania.

In the thirteenth and fourteenth centuries, local rulers invited German settlers to Poland, Bohemia, and Hungary. The superior German culture prompted Slavic rulers to bring in German peasantry and bourgeoisie. Pomerania was fully Germanized, and in Silesia, a state system was modeled on German governance. In Poland, German knights were granted large estates in fee, while German citizens founded the first Polish cities.[70] It did not take long before a network of German settlements spread across all of Poland. German was preached in the churches of Kraków and Lviv, court proceedings were held in German, and the University of Kraków functioned as a German institution in Polish lands.

---

[69] Livonia is a historical region on the northeastern shores of the Baltic Sea, comprising most of present-day Latvia and Estonia, while Prussia was on the southern shores of the Baltic. Samogitia is a region in modern Lithuania that separates Livonia and Prussia.

[70] Holding property "in fee" under feudal law refers to possessing property, typically land, with the obligation to provide feudal service to an overlord, with the right to pass the property to heirs.

The German influence in the regions around the Vistula River and Carpathian Mountains was so strong that it is fair to say this land was developed and civilized by Germans.

Sudeten Germans

Remnants of the German population had survived in Bohemia and Moravia. Under Charles IV, the region seemed entirely aligned with German culture. Invited by the king of Hungary, German peasants in Transylvania established their own communities, creating a robust German cultural presence that preserved its identity through seven centuries of conflict.

Rise of Poland and Hungary

The influx of German immigrants and their cultural contributions greatly strengthened the non-German states, particularly Poland and Hungary. With strong leadership, these nations achieved political unification. This inevitably led to a decline in the dominant German position in the east, as there was no unified German Reich or powerful monarchy to support the individual German states. Consequently, the decline of German political power was swift. The State of the Teutonic Order was encircled by the Polish-Lithuanian union formed in 1385 and suffered economic and political ruin after the Battle of Grunwald in 1410.

Hussite Separatism

In Bohemia, German influence suffered a severe blow due to the Hussite movement. The cultural contributions of the German population eventually provoked reactionary nationalism among Czech separatists, which manifested in the fervent religious and social movement associated with Jan Hus.[71] From the outset, this movement aimed to eliminate German dominance in the state, the Church, academia and the economy. The empire failed to quell the Bohemian separatism and was forced to grant it extensive political autonomy, leading to the emergence of a distinctly national Czech monarchy in 1458.[72] Thus, the region that had once been a focal point and stronghold for German influence in the east was now ruled by a Slavic presence openly opposed to all things German.

Germany's eastern front, which had previously been so powerful and ready to fight, had by the mid-fifteenth century been forced entirely into a defensive position; it was beginning to falter and, in some areas, suffer incursions.

The Threat in the West

Danger on Two Fronts

Around this time, a similar situation unfolded in the west. The geographical risk of a two-front war, a risk which had emerged during the formation of the empire—that is, the simultaneous threat from both the east and the west—resurfaced in full force in the fifteenth century and began to dominate the empire's situation.

A powerful state had formed on Germany's western border, just as the aging empire's power was waning. The rise of France as a military power immediately posed a threat to the empire's

---

[71] Jan Hus was a Czech revolutionary and theologian who opposed the dominant German influence in Bohemia, advocating for religious reform and greater Czech national identity, which ultimately led to his execution and the Hussite Wars.

[72] In 1458, George of Poděbrady was crowned king of Bohemia. He was celebrated as a "national" king for his efforts to defend Czech independence, promote religious tolerance among his people and reduce foreign influence in Bohemia.

borders, with ambitions to expand at the expense of Germany. Early on, French leaders began to have notions of the military frontiers the Kingdom of France should possess.

France Becomes a Great Power

As early as the fourteenth century, there was talk in France that the Rhine should be the boundary separating Germany from France. Alongside this, French kings sought to secure the German crown for themselves and their dynasty. Sadly, there was no fundamental opposition to such ambitions among the German princes, as their own local power was more important to them than the empire itself.

France's Advance Toward the Rhine

It is no surprise, then, that French advances were met with only weak resistance. The loss of German territory would have been even greater had it not been for France's own circumstances. The ongoing conflict with England, known as the Hundred Years' War, had long provided Germany with significant protection.[73] However, as that war drew to a close and England began to lose, the situation quickly changed. In 1444, the now-unengaged French army appeared in Lorraine and Alsace, demanding the submission of Metz and Strasbourg and launching an attack on Basel. Their withdrawal was eventually won after many negotiations and threats. But it was a close call—Alsace nearly became French at that time.

---

[73] The Hundred Years' War, initiated by English claims to the French throne, led to the expulsion of English forces from most of France and significantly altered the balance of power in Europe; the conflict protected German interests by diverting French military attention away from the Holy Roman Empire, thereby reducing French influence on Germany.

Burgundy Seeks To Expand its Territory

An even greater threat came from the newly formed Burgundian state, which emerged in 1384 from the political union of the Dutch counties with the County of Burgundy.[74] From the outset, Burgundy pursued a relentless expansion at the expense of the empire. The left bank of the Rhine was in danger, but it was not the empire that confronted this threat. Instead, a determined alliance of the affected Upper Rhine cities and lords, along with the Swiss, delivered a decisive blow, abruptly ending Burgundy's ambitions in Alsace and Lorraine. This may have been just an episode, but it staggeringly highlighted the empire's predicament: It was defenseless. And who could say whether the danger in the west had truly passed?

Fragmentation of Power in the Fifteenth Century

The problem of two fronts was especially dangerous for the empire at that time, as its internal power structure became increasingly fragmented. The available resources were not unified under a cohesive common purpose; in short, the empire was no longer united.

What Did the Empire Look Like in the Fifteenth Century?

The fifteenth century in Germany was a period of extreme fragmentation, marked by flourishing local states. The princes had triumphed over the knights and cities. However, the internal order of the empire did not become any less confusing or more stable with the rise of local powers. What the princes

---

[74] Burgundy was ruled by a noble house owing fealty to the Kings of France, thus, the expansion of Burgundian authority within the Empire threatened German influence in the west.

Medieval life in the fifteenth century

In the foreground, an itinerant journeyman and a merchant. In the background, traveling minstrels approach, begging money from the nobleman who is accompanied by armed guards.

gained in power, the king lost, leading to the monarchy's gradual decline into insignificance from the mid-fifteenth century onward. The princes claimed absolute power as local rulers, although their ulterior motive was to increase their own power and territory at the expense of their neighbors. This led to numerous hereditary feuds, especially concerning borders, such as those between the Palatinate and Bavaria, or Bavaria and the Hohenzollerns.[75]

Feuds Among Princes

Feuds characterized the political leadership of the nation, at a time when its position between its neighbors grew more precarious by the day. It is easy to understand why the empire had no coherent foreign policy under these circumstances: Its resources were consumed by internecine strife. Blinded by short-sighted pursuits of their own power, the princes had no sense of shared interest in the well-being of the empire. They were indifferent to the losses along the empire's western border, just as they were in the past to the subjugation of the Teutonic Order by Poland.

Power Politics of the Habsburgs

The empire had a king and emperor, who theoretically should have played the role of a central authority. However, nowhere is it more evident that theory and reality seldom agree. The ruling Habsburgs completely neglected their imperial duties, focusing solely on their own dynastic interests, much like the other princes. This shows how even the king had stopped thinking at a national level. He had become just another local

---

[75] The House of Hohenzollern was a distinguished German noble family that rose to prominence by ruling over Prussia and later establishing the German Empire in 1871.

ruler, using the imperial crown merely as a tool to advance his family's interests. Through marriages and testamentary contracts,[76] the Habsburgs were poised to gain control over Burgundy in the west and Hungary in the east—both without a single battle! The political marriages of the Habsburgs are famously captured in the adage, "Let others wage war; you, fortunate Austria, get married!"[77]

However, these ambitions of the Habsburgs entangled the empire in foreign affairs that ultimately brought nothing but the enmity of France and Hungary, as Austria also represented the imperial authority. The result of this policy was a shift in Germany's historical center of power from its traditional Germanic lands between the Rhine, Main, and Elbe rivers to the southeast, in which imperial powers were increasingly interested.

As history unfolded, this inner displacement of the empire proved to be a grave mistake, as it neglected its natural source of strength—one that, by its very development, had always been rooted in the ancient Germanic heartlands. The foundations of the Habsburg monarchy were distinctly Habsburg in nature and by no means German.

Habsburg's Dependence on the Pope

The Habsburgs thus gradually distanced themselves from Germany, despite holding the imperial title until 1806, and instead aligned themselves politically and religiously with

---

[76] Testamentary contracts in medieval law were legally binding agreements that allowed individuals to determine the distribution of their estate upon death, often overriding the traditional inheritance laws by specifying heirs and the attached conditions in advance.

[77] The adage is from a fourteenth-century couplet, originally in Latin: "Let others wage war; you, fortunate Austria, get married! / For what Mars gives to others, the goddess Venus gives to you." Mars was the Roman god of war, while Venus was the Roman goddess of love.

In a medieval printer's workshop

Rome and the Pope. As a result, an ongoing dualism—the Catholic Church on one side and the empire on the other—persisted within the German people, although the way this dualism manifested itself would change over time. The old emperors, as representatives of Germany in the world, had openly opposed the Pope, but that era had ended. The Habsburgs submitted to the political power of the Church with little resistance and eventually became obedient servants, so long as the Pope did not hinder their ambitions to expand their dynasty's power.

The Church had secured a political victory, gaining a firm foothold in Germany's development through its influence over the imperial house itself. The Habsburgs' leadership, which increasingly turned away from German interests, played into the Church's hands by further fragmenting the internal unity of the German people. The age-old Roman strategy of "divide and conquer" once again proved useful and effective for the Church.

During that time, German dualism appeared to be dormant, given the powerless state of the German people and lack of leadership. However, this lasted only until new forces emerged from within the people themselves, reigniting the struggle in a transformed, purely spiritual form. At that moment, the un-German stance of the Habsburgs became evident to all Germans, as the soul of the people stood in opposition to the rulers of the Holy Roman Empire of the German Nation.

The Development of German Intellectuals

The possibility of a unified German nation was thwarted by the emperors' stance on the question of German identity. As a result, the focus of German life and progress shifted to the individual states over the following centuries. This ushered in a turbulent and restless era, in which the German spirit became increasingly fragmented, ultimately to the detriment of the people, because of the lack of strong leadership.

Cultural Nourishment for the World

Germany's tragic fate during this period, and for some time afterward, was to contribute new ideas to the cultural world in every field of intellectual life, while politically sinking into ever deeper weakness. The German people, decomposing in their afflictions, became the fertile ground from which the world's culture flourished, even as they themselves withered away.

During this period of political crisis, the German people sought to numb their inner turmoil and national pain by channeling their intellectual and artistic energies into remarkable achievements. With the invention of the printing press, Germany had a tool that made it possible for even the broader public to engage with intellectual creation and cultural developments. This era marked a resurgence of the German spirit, as it strove, generation after generation, to create something greater and to seek even higher forms of expression. The names that have gone down in the annals of German literature and art at the beginning of the sixteenth century bear witness to this: Sebastian Brant, Hans Sachs, Albrecht Dürer, Lucas Cranach, Matthias Grünewald, Hans Holbein, Veit Stoss, and Tilman Riemenschneider—all of whom exemplified the unique character of the German people through their contributions to literature and art. Albrecht Dürer's engraving *Knight, Death, and the Devil* stands as a powerful symbol of the German nation itself.[78]

However, it was not just visual art and literature that experienced a golden age at that time; architecture also underwent a renaissance, reflected in the grand construction of ornate castles and the beautifully crafted timber-framed town halls and guildhalls.

In every aspect, there was a fresh and invigorating sense of national identity. People peered into Germany's past to prove that the Germans had always been a people of great feats and achievements, equal to any other; they knew what they could accomplish under better circumstances.

Culturally Flourishing but Politically Powerless

The yawning chasm between reality and the ideal caused deep unease among intellectuals. The prouder one felt of Germany's heritage and its inherent worth, the more acutely one perceived the Germans' low standing among the nations. The reason for this was clear: While neighboring countries had organized themselves into strong nation-states, the Germans lacked such a nation-state. The German constitution was inadequate; it left the empire powerless externally and drained its internal strength

---

[78] *Knight, Death, and the Devil* is a copper engraving from 1513 which depicts a resolute armored knight riding through a dark and foreboding landscape, flanked by personifications of Death and the Devil. It has profoundly influenced the German nation by symbolizing the moral strength, perseverance and resolve that became central themes in German cultural and national identity during the Renaissance and beyond. It was highly idealized during the National Socialist era in Germany.

with feuds and unrest. No one was satisfied with this constitution: not the emperor because it offered him no means of power, not the princes because it did not grant them sufficient influence and not the people because the empire, in its current form, was no match for its neighbors and faced a precarious future.

Wars of Religion

Luther's Struggle Against Rome

A second crisis, far deeper in impact, had just erupted with the beginning of Charles V's reign—the religious crisis.[79] This was not unique to Germany, as all of Western Christendom experienced it, but it first broke out in Germany, where it had the most profound and lasting effects. Martin Luther's historical significance lies in his immortal achievement of standing against spiritual and mental enslavement, against priestly tyranny, arbitrary rule, and exploitation. It is important to recall that the struggle between the empire and the papacy, the battle for political and spiritual leadership, had ended with the triumph of Rome's claim to power. However, with that victory, the victor lost his moral integrity.

Even though the German Reich under imperial leadership had been defeated, the morally corrupt Church was bound to encounter resistance from forces that had remained strong and alive within the uncorrupted German people.

It is telling and evocative of the National Socialist doctrine of blood and soil that the man who reignited the struggle against the political power of the Catholic Church,

---

[79] Charles V was Holy Roman Emperor, reigning from 1519 to 1556, and presided over an expansive empire spanning Europe and the Americas, including being king of Spain through dynastic inheritance. He played a pivotal role in the religious and political conflicts of the Reformation.

Lucas Cranach the Elder and Albrecht Dürer, two German masters of painting

albeit in a different and purely spiritual fashion, came from a long-established peasant family in Thuringia. Luther was a revolutionary German leader who, by creating a unified form of written German, was able to address the entire nation.[80]

Ecclesiastical Corruption

The Church's corruption was evident in the moral decay of its leaders, both in Rome and in Germany, as well as in the shameless way faith in God was exploited for profit. The extravagant lifestyles of the ecclesiastical princes, whose episcopal courts resembled more a venue for furtive orgies

---

[80] Much like the King James Bible did for English, Martin Luther's German translation of the Bible, first published in 1522, was highly influential in standardizing the written form of the German language, as it provided a more accessible and unifying text that shaped written German and contributed to its development as a more consistent and uniform language across different regions.

than a center of cultural patronage, were well known to the people who languished in bitter poverty. This they observed with grim resentment and deep anger.

Other States Leave the Catholic Church

In addition to this, there was something unique to Germany. The Catholic Church had always been a centralized monarchy under the Pope as the absolute ruler. From Rome, the churches of all countries were governed and exploited as Rome saw fit. However, during the Reformation, this central control was significantly curtailed for countries beyond Germany. In England, France, Spain, and even Italy, the civil authorities were able to protect their interests according to their local circumstances. Everywhere, nations had become the masters of their own ecclesiastical affairs. It was up to them to decide how much they were willing to concede to a foreign power like the Pope.

This had also been the goal in Germany, but it was not achieved because the country lacked a strong centralized secular authority that could effectively stand up to the Pope.

Germany as Rome's Source of Revenue

As the independence of western countries grew, the Pope's revenue from those regions diminished. Naturally, the Church sought income from elsewhere and found it in Germany. The Pope himself referred to the Germans as "the most faithful children of the Roman Church."[81] The less France and England contributed, the more Germany was burdened. A favored method of extracting money was through the sale of

---

[81] This exact quotation is not attributable to any specific pope or document; nonetheless, Germans were considered among the most loyal supporters of the Catholic Church in the Middle Ages.

indulgences, which would have been scarcely permitted in other countries. In Germany, however, permission could be easily bought from local rulers by offering them a share of the profits, a practice that was eagerly pursued.

Germany Rises Up Against the Exploitation

This situation was deeply felt. The disparity between the treatment received by Germany and the consideration shown to other countries was evident, leading to a strong sense of oppression and exploitation. The awakening national identity began to turn against Rome. The growing criticism of the clergy, along with the rejection of their privileged status, was intertwined with resentment toward the papal court, seen as the foreign power oppressing and exploiting the German people. Complaints against Roman authority were a constant refrain at the Imperial Diet.[82]

Rome was seen as the enemy of the German nation—if not the only one, then certainly the main one. This sentiment found its most eloquent expression in the polemical writings of the German fighter Ulrich von Hutten.[83] However, the debates at the Imperial Diet did nothing to improve these conditions. It was likely a situation similar to what we experienced during the fourteen years of parliamentary rule before the Führer took over leadership of the Reich.

---

[82] The Imperial Diet was the central deliberative assembly of the Holy Roman Empire where its princes and leaders met to discuss and make decisions on key issues, including religious matters, such as in 1521 when it condemned Martin Luther for his role in the Reformation.

[83] Ulrich von Hutten was a German reformer, humanist and outspoken critic of the Catholic Church, whose writings and advocacy for religious and political change made him a key figure in the early stages of the Protestant Reformation in Germany.

Luther's Struggle Against a Foreign Power

Luther took up the fight against Rome with relentless determination, unaware of the full impact it would have. His thoughts, feelings, will and actions were deeply rooted in the people, which is why he felt the foreign domination of his people so acutely. Luther's struggle was focused on the preservation of German identity and the liberation of the German soul from the foreign Mediterranean power.

Anyone who sees Luther merely as the founder of a non-Catholic denomination fails to understand him. We recognize him not just as the founder of Protestantism but as one of the greatest "protesters" in the entirety of German history—indeed, the most significant figure in that ongoing protest against superstition and priestly domination, a protest that has repeatedly surged forth from the depths of the Germanic essence of our people with unstoppable force.

Luther and the German People

How did the German people respond to Luther's bold struggle? The majority of the people saw in him not just the promise of a religious renewal and a correction of the Church's abuses, but indeed hoped for something far greater. Amid the turbulence and fervor of the time, the deep longing of the people for an authentically German identity, a sweeping reform of the empire, and the establishment of a just system aligned with their cultural values stood as the driving force behind all their desires. The time had come, they believed, for liberation from their national plight, something that had not been achieved in the chaos of scattered peasant revolts, in the storming of monasteries, or in the burning of castles.

Luther Was no Political Leader

It was Germany's great misfortune that Luther did not, and could not, fulfill the hopes of the German people in this regard, for he lacked the gift of political leadership.

Luther Standardizes Written German

One of Luther's lasting achievements is the creation of a standard written language for all of Germany. In an era when only those who knew Latin could read and write, this was the most crucial step in preserving German identity.

Ulrich von Hutten

Alongside the freedom fighter Luther stands another warrior of a different kind: Ulrich von Hutten. The scion of a well-known noble family, Hutten was a knight, orator, man of the people, writer, painter, prophet, and above all, a fighter.

Hutten is remembered in our people's history as a champion of freedom, justice, and honor. While Luther's main concern was, "How do I find a gracious God?" Hutten asked, "How do I create a free German nation?"

Hutten's significance is only now truly being recognized, as he was barely given any attention during his own era. He left virtually no mark on his contemporaries and had no influence on the political developments of his day. In fact, Luther, who was unsettled by Hutten's forceful pen and impetuous nature, distanced himself from him and refused to collaborate with him.

Peasants' War

The unrest among peasants during the Reformation was closely tied to Luther's movement. Although there had been earlier scattered attempts by the peasantry to revive ancient Germanic traditions and heritage, such as the Stedinger revolt against the Church,[84] the Peasants' War was a widespread signal of deep-seated discontent.[85] This unrest was ignited by Luther's fundamentally Nordic resistance to the foreign nature of the Catholic Church.

History of the Peasantry

If we want to fully grasp the dreadful impact of the Peasants' War on Germany, a brief historical overview is necessary. Luther's proclamation of the freedom of the Christian citizen stirred the entire German populace into rebellion against Rome. The Reformation had swept triumphantly across the German land. The leaders of the German peasantry saw this as the opportune moment to demand the reinstatement of their ancient rights. Until then, the Catholic Church, despite occasional political defeats, had prevailed over the peasantry in social and spiritual matters.

Peasants Deprived of Their Rights

The agrarian system of old was based on freedom and communal tribal property, with minimal social distinctions. However, Rome and the Christian Church dismantled Germanic inheritance laws. Since the introduction of Christianity, individuals were encouraged to dispose of their property for the salvation of their souls, often at the expense of the clan. Rome and the Christian Church also facilitated the rise of the manorial system, which gradually replaced

---

[84] The Stedinger revolt was a thirteenth-century uprising by the peasants of Stedingen in Northern Germany against the excessive demands of local nobles and the archbishop, ultimately leading to the peasants' defeat in 1234 with a crusade sanctioned by Pope Gregory IX.

[85] The German Peasants' War was a large-scale uprising by peasants in the Holy Roman Empire, driven by grievances over heavy taxation, feudal oppression and demands for religious and economic reforms heavily influenced by the Reformation; it ultimately ended in defeat for the peasants.

The peasant awakens!

free ownership by peasants, reducing them only to serfdom and subjugation.[86]

Later, the land was divided into smaller estates, particularly under the control of the Church and the lower nobility. Peasants were obligated to do corvée or pay taxes, while some free peasants

---

[86] The manorial system was the dominant economic, political and social institution of medieval Europe, where feudal lords controlled large estates and the peasantry, often bound as serfs, lived under strict obligations to provide labor, goods and services to their lord in exchange for protection and the right to farm small plots of land, typically under harsh conditions with limited personal freedoms.

still existed, although they too were politically disenfranchised.[87] Meanwhile, the clergy, nobility, and bourgeoisie retained or even gained political influence. Peasants were barred from rising to the rank of knighthood and from bearing arms, effectively relegating them to the disenfranchised fourth estate.

Peasantry Fights Back

As the feudal state evolved into a territorial state dominated by princes in the late Middle Ages, the peasantry, inspired by Luther's message of the "freedom of a Christian,"[88] sought to overthrow the territorialization of the empire through the Peasants' War, aiming to establish a new empire founded on free peasant communities. This revolt failed because of the resistance of the local princes, who, to the detriment of the empire and German unity, emerged victorious. This caused the empire to fragment into multiple states, a situation that was only truly overcome by National Socialism.[89] Despite their uprisings, such as the major Austrian peasant revolts led by Stefan Fadinger, Michael Gaismair, and other peasant leaders, the peasants ultimately became subjects under the ruling classes.[90]

---

[87] Corvée was a form of forced labor in medieval Europe where peasants were required to work on their lord's land or perform other services without pay, as part of their obligations under the manorial system.

[88] *On the Freedom of a Christian* is a treatise written by Martin Luther in 1520.

[89] This situation is sometimes referred to today as *Kleinstaaterei*, a term that denotes the historical fragmentation of Germany into numerous small, independent states and principalities, which persisted well into the nineteenth century, leading to political disunity and the delayed unification of the German nation. At its height in the eighteenth century, there were more than three hundred of these independent states.

[90] One such revolt was the Upper Austrian peasant war of 1626 during the Thirty Years' War, driven by dissatisfaction with Catholic rulers and harsh economic conditions, ultimately resulting in the peasants' defeat by imperial forces. Stefan Fadinger and Michael Gaismair were prominent leaders of peasant revolts in Austria and Tyrol, respectively, both advocating for economic and social reforms, with Fadinger leading the Upper Austrian peasant war and Gaismair promoting a radical vision of social change within the wider context of the Reformation.

Luther's Stance on the Peasant Revolts

A major reason for the failure of the peasant revolts was Luther's treatise *Against the Murderous, Thieving Hordes of Peasants,* in which he sided with the local princes. This decision cost Luther much of his support among the people. Moreover, the peasant movement lacked the organization and strength needed to succeed.

Without any conscious or coordinated leadership, the peasant revolts erupted in various places. What started as isolated fires quickly grew into a blazing inferno, spreading from Austria through Bavaria, Swabia and all the way up to the Harz Mountains. Although the peasants' cause was deeply rooted and justifiable, it was politically doomed given the circumstances. The empire and its princes were the dominant powers of the sixteenth century, and a major decisive battle was already underway between them.

Tragedy of the Peasants' War and the Knights' War

The tragedy of the Peasants' War is that, around the same time but separate from the peasants, the knights staged their own uprising with the goal of reorganizing Germany, overthrowing the princes and establishing a new social order. The knights could have led the peasant movement, but they were only interested in reforms that excluded peasants from political involvement. Very few knights aligned themselves with the peasants, as they failed to realize the deep misery and plight of the impoverished peasants.

The Knights' War, led by Franz von Sickingen and Ulrich von Hutten, failed because they did not understand the true demands of the time and were only interested in restoring knighthood to its former state. Had these two forces—knights and peasants— united in a common cause, establishing a new vision for the empire might have been more easily achieved.

Immense Loss of Life

The failure of the uprising, which drained the peasantry of its best blood, along with the heavy losses brought about by the subsequent Thirty Years' War, left the peasant class so weakened that it no longer had any influence in politics. It was not until Adolf Hitler's new Reich that the peasantry was restored to its rightful position as the backbone of the nation.

Counter-Reformation and the Jesuit Order

As the Reformation was sweeping triumphantly across Germany —at that time, seven-eighths of the population in what is now Catholic Austria were Protestant—the Jesuit order was founded in Spain. Its mission was not only to halt the decline of the papacy, and thus the Catholic Church, but also to revitalize it and reclaim large parts of its lost territory. Unfortunately, the Germans, specifically the Habsburgs, played a regrettable role in this re-Catholicization. As a result, sharply divided states with different religious affiliations emerged within the empire, permanently solidifying the split in the German people. By 1600, the religious boundaries were largely set in place, shaping the landscape of our fatherland to this day.

Even today, Luther is often blamed for causing a religious schism within Germany. However, if there were a schism or religious war, it was not Luther's fault but rather the powers—like the Jesuit order and the princes who followed them—that stopped the Reformation from reaching its natural conclusion, in which the last remaining Catholic minority would have converted to Protestantism. Germany was on the path to religious unity, and it was the Counter-Reformation that caused the schism.

The incessant pressure from Rome eventually led to the division of Germany into two political and religious factions, between which only armed conflict could settle the fight.

Germany, the Playground of Europe

The Thirty Years' War is perhaps the darkest chapter in German history. Beyond the horrifying depopulation—Germany's population fell from around twenty million to just five million—and the devastation of its territory, there is another tragedy: Germany, once the pinnacle of a glorious medieval empire, had fallen so low that, already politically and ideologically fractured, it became an object of foreign powers' politics and a battlefield for the conflicts of other European states.

This brutal conflict was driven by the political ambitions of France and the Catholic Church, both aiming to eradicate the unique racial and spiritual identity of the German people. What began as a religious dispute over dogma quickly escalated into a campaign of extermination against the Nordic race, with Germans as its primary representatives. Every other race and every method of devastation, including destruction, murder, and arson, was mobilized to achieve this goal.

Germany After 1648

Germany Helpless as its European Neighbors
Grow Stronger

The empire, consumed by its pursuit of an all-embracing realm and its struggles against the papacy, drained the best of its national strength, neglected the most pressing issues within its own territory and allowed local rulers to gain greater autonomy as imperial authority began to erode. While Germany once eclipsed other nations at its zenith, the following centuries marked its decline, as England, France, and Spain rose to become strong nation-states.

What, then, was the result of the Thirty Years' War?

Consequences of the Thirty Years' War

Germany had been reduced to a wasteland. Famine, disease, and other scourges—along with their devastating consequences—had decimated the population. On top of this came the contamination of the Nordic lineage: For thirty years, Spanish, Italian, Czech, French, and Hungarian mercenaries had roamed through Germany, savagely raping its women and girls.

Germany had been set back centuries, and it would take many years before the sense of being German could once again be felt as a source of pride.

Peace of Westphalia

The Peace of Westphalia, which ended the Thirty Years' War, brought no resolution to the ideological or religious divides. Germany remained split into two hostile camps, with local rulers continuing to dictate the religion of their subjects. Religious persecution did not cease, but persisted well into the following century, fostering divisions that took root so deeply in the German people that they remain a challenge to overcome even to this day.

Loss of Territory

The Peace of Westphalia also dealt a severe blow to Germany's political strength. Switzerland and the Dutch Republic were recognized as independent states, thus seceding from the Holy Roman Empire. France gained the three bishoprics of Toul, Metz, and Verdun in Lorraine, along with Upper Alsace and various rights in Lower Alsace. Thus, France's "traditional" or "classical"

Rhine policy began to take concrete shape in 1648.[91]

Sweden was granted Western Pomerania and the bishoprics of Verden and Bremen, giving it control over the mouths of the Oder, Elbe, and Weser rivers. Consequently, the outlets of all major German rivers now fell into foreign hands. (See Map 13.)

Additionally, with the loss of its coastline, Germany forfeited any opportunity to partake in the global exploration and conquest that unfolded over the following decades and centuries. While France, England, and the Netherlands established vast colonial empires, Germany made no moves to claim its share of the world's wealth—apart from the tentative efforts of the Great Elector.[92] The division of the globe occurred entirely without the participation of the Holy Roman Empire or the German people. Rome had achieved its goal.

Germany in Fragments

France and Sweden were among the signatories to the Peace of Westphalia and thus became guarantors of all its provisions. This meant that these foreign powers assumed the authority to oversee and ensure the sovereignty of the numerous German principalities, both large and small—a situation so romantically

---

[91] France's "traditional" or "classical" Rhine policy refers to its long-standing strategic objective of establishing the Rhine as its eastern frontier, dating back to the reign of Louis XIV and continuing through the Napoleonic era. This policy sought to expand French territory and influence by controlling the Rhine as a natural defensive barrier and an economic and political axis, often at the expense of the German states, and it shaped much of France's military and diplomatic efforts in Europe during the early modern period.

[92] Frederick William, Elector of Brandenburg and Duke of Prussia, is popularly known as the Great Elector. Despite his shrewd political achievements and military prowess, he had modest colonial ambitions and only engaged in limited forays into the Atlantic slave trade. By 1871, when Germany was unified under the German Empire, none of its constituent states had any overseas colonies and there was only a minimal history of colonial projects.

Map 13: Germany after 1648

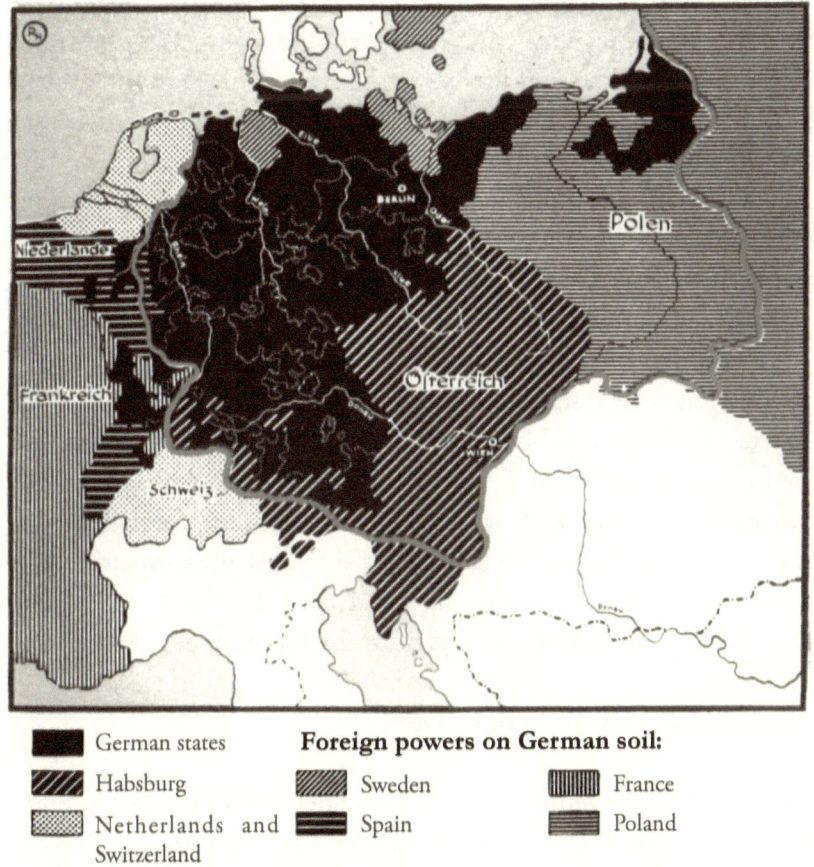

■ German states	**Foreign powers on German soil:**	
▨ Habsburg	▨ Sweden	▥ France
▦ Netherlands and Switzerland	▬ Spain	▤ Poland

The Thirty Years' War left Germany in devastating ruin, but the political consequences were even more dire: Foreign powers now controlled German territory. Switzerland and the Netherlands became independent, while the Holy Roman Empire itself was rendered powerless, at the mercy of foreign powers.

Sweden seized Western Pomerania and the Archbishopric of Bremen, stripping Germany of the vital mouths of the Weser, Elbe, and Oder rivers, in addition to the already lost Rhine delta.

France annexed the bishoprics of Lorraine and significant portions of Alsace, signaling its renewed claim to the left bank of the Rhine.

referred to as "German liberty."[93] In reality, this arrangement granted them the ability to interfere in the internal affairs of the German people at any time, effectively ensuring the continued helplessness of the empire and the fragmentation of Central Europe. This state of division became the foundation of their own security and power. From this point forward, any attempt to solve the "German question" was inevitably both a German and a European issue. It was evident that the other European powers would resist any change to the status quo established in 1648, especially if it aimed at German unity.[94]

The Thirty Years' War offers a grim lesson about the fate of a nation that tears itself apart with internal conflict, becoming an easy target for its neighbors while its land serves as a battleground for foreign interests. At the time, it seemed as though Germany's end was imminent, with its final partition among foreign powers only a matter of time. Yet fate had a different plan for us, as one thing survived the suffering and death, the horror and devastation: the indomitable spirit of the German people.

German Peasantry Defends its Land

Although foreign blood may have mingled with ours and the loss of German lives may have been staggeringly high, the core of our people endured. This resilience is owed to the quiet heroism of countless unknown Germans—above all, to the German peasantry. Despite unspeakable suffering and hardship, they

---

[93] "German liberty" was a political principle in the Holy Roman Empire that championed the autonomy and sovereignty of the Empire's constituent states, safeguarding their rights against centralization by the emperor and becoming a defining feature of the Empire's decentralized structure. Unfortunately, this "liberty" became so extreme that it allowed for the constituent states to effectively become colonies of foreign powers.

[94] The so-called "German Question" was focused on the best way to unify the German-speaking world. Other European powers opposed unification in an attempt to preserve their own power and prevent the rise of a dominant Germany.

remained steadfast on their land, tirelessly restoring devastated fields and ensuring the survival of our nation.

Because they remained loyal to themselves, their people, and their land, it became possible, one day, for a new German Reich to rise from the ruins of the old, after the political collapse of 1648. This new Reich found its inspiration and unification taking shape even then, in the aftermath of the long war, within one of the German states: Brandenburg-Prussia.Brandenburg-Prussia[95]

Beginning of a New Reich

This state, emerging from the humblest beginnings in a land not generously endowed by nature, rose to impressive heights under Frederick the Great. It was destined to uphold the German spirit during a time when the old Reich lay in ruins. Thirty years of devastation had shattered the already fragile structure of the Holy Roman Empire. The Habsburg dynasty, long uninterested in Germany's fate, now lacked the political strength to reorganize the land. Every small-time petty local ruler sought to expand his own domain; the era of German fragmentation and division was inaugurated.

German identity had disintegrated, with people affiliating more with their region than with Germany. The memory of Germany's once-mighty empire lingered only as a distant dream, buried deep in the hearts of a few patriotic Germans, yet still unreal and devoid of any tangible hope for revival.

---

[95] Keeping track of the various men named "Frederick" and their titles in this section can be confusing. As a family line, Frederick William, Elector of Brandenburg (also known as the Great Elector), is the starting point here. His son is Frederick I of Prussia (also known as Frederick III of Brandenburg). His son is Frederick William I of Prussia (also called the Soldier King). His son is Frederick II of Prussia, later known as Frederick the Great. Also, bear in mind that the text is not strictly chronological. For instance, in one paragraph, it may be discussing Frederick the Great, and in the next, it jumps to Frederick William and then to Frederick William I; the focus is more on the theme rather than the chronology of events.

The Great Elector

Brandenburg Versus Habsburg

In this time of profound crisis, all eyes turned to Brandenburg-Prussia, which had grown under the Great Elector into the strongest state in Northern Germany. It was the best governed, most enterprising, and truly the preeminent state among German Protestants. The Habsburgs began to view this rising power with envy, even going so far as to align themselves with France and Sweden when Brandenburg, justifiably, laid claim to Pomerania following its victory over Sweden at Fehrbellin. The Austro-Prussian rivalry became increasingly apparent. Meanwhile, a strengthened France skillfully exploited this power struggle, steadily advancing along the western borders of the Reich to secure its own gains.

Map 14: Prussia and Austria in the Eighteenth Century

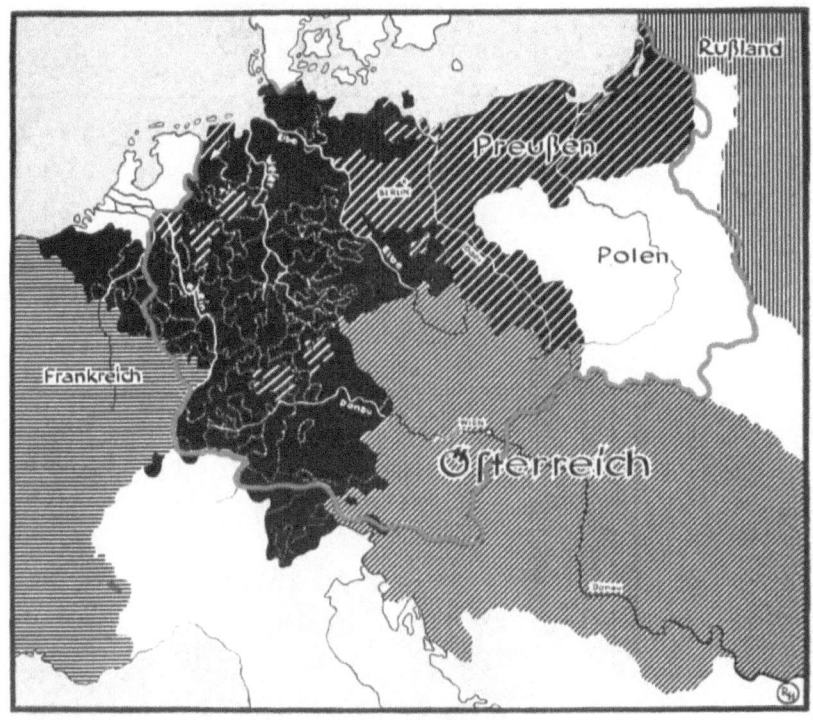

▇ German states

From humble beginnings, Prussia gradually rose to prominence under Frederick the Great, establishing itself alongside the aging Austria as the most powerful force in the German-speaking world. In stark contrast, the rest of the Holy Roman Empire remained a fragmented patchwork of various small states.

Frederick William Builds Up Brandenburg

At this stage, Brandenburg-Prussia was not yet ready to challenge Austria in armed conflict. However, Frederick William, through his years of leadership, had developed the foresight to understand that preparing for such a confrontation was an essential part of his mission for Germany. His vision and ambitions extended far beyond Brandenburg's borders, always focused on the greater cause of Germany.

His greatness lies in having established the framework for the House of Hohenzollern to lead Germany and in building the political power necessary to realize this goal. Tirelessly dedicated to the welfare of his land and the advancement of his people, he restored security, confidence, and a renewed sense of national pride to the people under his rule.

Frederick William I, the Soldier King

Support for the Peasantry

As a great organizer, he also understood the critical importance of a strong and healthy peasantry for the survival of a nation. In the Altmark and along the lowlands of the Oder, Havel, and Warta rivers, he initiated large-scale drainage projects to transform swampy areas into fertile farmland. Then, he encouraged retired soldiers to settle on this reclaimed land.

Formation of a Standing Army

Furthermore, he laid the foundation for the establishment of the Prussian state by creating a strong military force. The scattered regiments of mercenaries and officers, who had previously served under their colonels as private contractors in a fragmented military system, were transformed into a standing, salaried, centrally organized state army under the direct command of the Great Elector.

Despite the political dependence on foreign subsidies, the resolute will of the Great Elector always remained internally independent and focused. As Frederick the Great aptly remarked, he was "the architect of Brandenburg's power."[96]

To the power he already inherited, Frederick III, Elector of Brandenburg, added additional prestige by obtaining the royal crown of Prussia. However, the crown proved too heavy for the young state. The task at hand was to harden and strengthen its foundations, laying the groundwork that would ultimately give the Prussian monarchy its true purpose and legitimacy.

---

[96] This is an excerpt from *Denkwürdigkeiten zur Geschichte des Hauses Brandenburg* ("Memoirs of the House of Brandenburg"), a work written in 1748 by Frederick the Great, the great-grandson of Frederick William.

The Soldier King Seeks Absolute Power

This monumental task fell to Frederick William I, the Soldier King. He was destined to live a life of preparation, amassing strength for a future generation. Prussia owes him the establishment of an unusually large standing army of eighty-three thousand soldiers, supported by an administration marked by exemplary discipline, frugality, and expertise. One trait sets him apart from all his contemporaries: his diligent sense of duty. He did not see himself as the master of his state, but as its servant.

Frederick William I through his actions already epitomized the famous remark of his son: that the king is the first servant of his state.[97] His work laid the firm foundation for the policies of his successor. Aware that the full significance of his life's efforts would only be realized after his time, he quietly but faithfully helped build Prussia's greatness, brick by brick. In his own way, this king aspired to what is demanded by National Socialism today: the total state.[98] For him, the basis was royal authority; for National Socialism, it is the people.

---

[97] The famous remark was made by Frederick the Great in his 1777 work *Regierungsformen und Herrscherpflichten* ("Forms of Government and the Ruler's Duties"), in which he explains the ruler "is merely the first servant of the state and is obliged to act with integrity, wisdom and complete selflessness, as though he were accountable at any moment to his fellow citizens for his administration."

[98] The "total state" is a concept that underpins National Socialist political theory. It was perhaps most notably expounded by Carl Schmitt, a leading jurist in Germany, in his 1933 work *Staat, Bewegung, Volk* ("State, Movement, People"). He portrayed the total state as an entity that should act concretely to unify its people rather than operate on abstract legal principles. Schmitt identified ethnic, religious and class diversity and equality as the greatest ills of society. He viewed the total state, and by extension National Socialism, as having "the courage to treat unequal things unequally and to enforce necessary differentiations." These arguments would ultimately serve as the legal basis for the Third Reich.

Frederick the Great Stands as a Shining Example

In Frederick II, the son of the Soldier King, the political will that had already thrived in the Great Elector came to life with its full original strength.

Frederick the Great's Foreign Policy

When Frederick assumed power, Prussia's foreign-policy stagnation came to an end. He sought to increase Prussia's power and prestige, intending to elevate it to the status of a European great power. The death of Holy Roman Emperor Charles VI, the last male Habsburg, brought two major issues to the forefront: the election of a new emperor and the question of the Habsburg patrimony. This presented an opportunity for Austria's ambitious neighbor. Frederick demanded the long-disputed territory of Silesia from Maria Theresa.[99] This bold move, breaking the peace of the old Reich, revealed a decisive political will aimed at establishing an independent and secure power base in Northern Germany.

Comparing Prussia and Austria

The Silesian Wars ensued, with Frederick emerging victorious in all three. The key outcome of these wars was the establishment of Prussia as a formidable power, rising to a level that not only matched but even surpassed the Austrian imperial authority within the Reich. From the outset, it was evident which of the two rivals would ultimately prevail.

Austria was a colorful mosaic, a conglomerate of European

---

[99] Silesia was an affluent province in the Habsburg dominions. With the death of Charles VI, Maria Theresa became the queen of Bohemia (among other titles), thus overseeing Silesia. Frederick the Great invaded and took the territory within approximately two months of the death of Charles VI.

Frederick the Great

states lacking stability and internal unity. On all sides, it was fraught with international tension: In Belgium and Italy, it was constantly at odds with France; along the Lower Danube, it faced conflicts with Russia and the Ottoman Empire. As a result, Austria was forced into cosmopolitan power politics, devoid of national focus and lacking the resources to sustain such a strategy.

In contrast stood Prussia—tightly unified, advancing in every field, and predominantly German in its population. Its borders safeguarded not only its own interests but also those of the German people. On the Lower Rhine, it countered France; in the east, it stood firm against Poland and Russia. With careful strategy and execution, Prussia was destined to prevail.

The attack Frederick launched against the old imperial house was unprecedented, catching the Austrians entirely off guard. It was an act of genius by someone who stands outside the bounds of ordinary progress, someone who is capable of greater ambition and achievement than the average person. This is the sort of person who shapes the course of history with sheer force of will. This decision set the trajectory for German history, a path it has followed to this day and will likely continue on in the future.

Prussia the Military State

The Prussian state introduced something entirely new to German history, not only by shifting the balance of power through its expansion but also through its very nature: It was a military state at its core.

All German states at the time maintained standing armies, and while Prussia's army was larger and more efficient than the others, this alone was not what set it apart. What distinguished Prussia significantly was that its army was funded entirely by the state's own resources. Driven by a commitment to frugality, Frederick William ensured that a substantial portion of its support came directly from the country itself.

Frederick the Great Lays the Groundwork for Modern Conscription

Frederick the Great was able to prosecute his lengthy wars with soldiers largely drawn from his own people. These native recruits proved far more reliable than foreign mercenaries, who were prone to desertion. This approach was unprecedented at the time, effectively laying the groundwork for modern conscription.[100]

As a result, Prussia's population developed a unique bond with the state, unlike anywhere else. This was particularly evident during the Seven Years' War.[101] Despite the immense hardships, there was no betrayal or defection; the people willingly and selflessly gave their all for their king and—for the first time one could rightfully use the term—for their fatherland. At last, there was a German state that its citizens could truly regard as their fatherland. Prussia's glory inspired faith in the coming resurgence of German greatness, awakening hopes for a renewed Germany under Prussian leadership.

Frederick's distinctly Nordic character was evident in his relentless drive. Even after achieving his goal—the permanent acquisition of Silesia for Prussia—he did not simply rest on his laurels, but immediately sought and embraced a new mission: rebuilding the lands devastated by the protracted war. He oversaw the cultivation of the Oderbruch,[102] provided state funds for reconstruction, distributed seeds from state granaries, and granted tax relief to those who had suffered losses during the war.

---

[100] This paragraph is likely referring to the Prussian canton system, which organized local populations to provide a steady supply of recruits for the Prussian Army, ensuring a disciplined and permanent military force. While it was first introduced by Frederick the Great's father toward the end of his life, Frederick the Great implemented a number of reforms to improve the system. The canton system was a precursor to modern conscription.

[101] The Seven Years' War was a global conflict over territorial disputes in Europe, particularly Austria's attempt to reclaim Silesia from Prussia, ultimately reshaping the balance of power in Europe and overseas. Great Britain and her colonies took the side of Prussia, while France and Russia joined the Austrians.

[102] The Oderbruch is a low-lying marshland along the Oder River in Eastern Germany, which Frederick the Great transformed into arable farmland through extensive drainage and reclamation projects, fostering settlement and agricultural development.

Prussia Is Germany

With the annexation of West Prussia, Warmia, and the Netze District, Prussia gained a more consolidated domain, now strategically oriented to the east.[103] This development also served one of the nation's greatest goals: reclaiming lost territory. In this sense, Prussian and German interests coincided seamlessly. (See Map 14.)

Prussian Sense of Honor

As an enlightened and independent thinker, Frederick the Great understood that the Prussian sense of honor—carried back from the bloody battlefields of the Seven Years' War as the army's most cherished possession—had to become a defining trait of the entire nation if Prussia was to endure through the ages. Only free, upright and morally steadfast individuals could bear the future of this embattled and envied state, a state destined to carry the German Reich into a new era.

Nonetheless, a potential risk lay in the powerful state built by Frederick the Great. Prussia's status as a great power was entirely the personal creation of Frederick himself. The legacy of a genius, unfortunately, often sets a standard that proves exceedingly difficult for successors to match. Similarly, Bismarck's achievements faced jeopardy, because those who followed lacked the strength and vision required to preserve and develop the newly established order.

Frederick's Weak Successors

---

103 West Prussia, Warmia and the Netze District were territories acquired by Frederick the Great during the First Partition of Poland in 1772, strategically securing a land bridge between East Prussia and Brandenburg, expanding Prussian control over key trade routes and enhancing its influence in Central Europe.

The successors of Frederick the Great were utterly unfit for the challenges of their time. They basked in the glory of the great king without understanding that a new era was dawning, one that would soon throw Europe into a whirlwind of upheaval and change.

The Downfall of Prussia

Napoleon and Germany

When Napoleon crowned himself Emperor of the French, thereby putting an end to the French Revolution, he recognized the decrepit state of the old German Reich under the Habsburgs, whose leadership had descended into criminal negligence. He also instinctively sensed the stagnation of Prussia, trapped in a superficial adherence to the legacy of Frederick the Great. Napoleon understood that the French Revolution had ushered in a new era, one that demanded sweeping transformations in every aspect of life. This upheaval was inevitable, for the eternal law of humanity is not stagnation but continuous progress.

Thus, it came to pass that just twenty years after the death of Frederick the Great, the Prussian state collapsed—not under the weight of some inescapable fate nor solely owing to its internal flaws and shortcomings, but through the failings of its leaders, in the truest sense. The incompetence, weakness, and negligence of its rulers and statesmen were to blame for its downfall.

The Holy Roman Empire Falls in 1806

In 1805, at the Battle of Austerlitz[104], Napoleon shattered the remnants of the old German Reich, which had at least formally existed until then. The expansive Southern German states declared

---

[104] 2 December 1805

Map 15: Germany under Napoleon in 1812

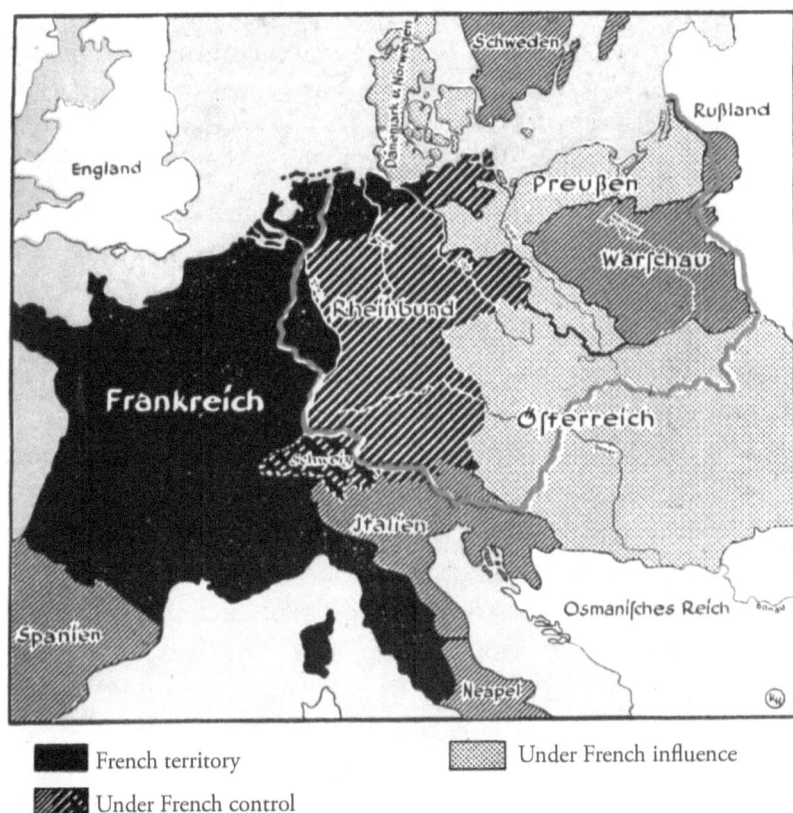

French territory

Under French control

Under French influence

Under Napoleon's onslaught, the old Reich was formally dissolved in 1806. In the newly established Confederation of the Rhine, German princes sold their allegiance to Napoleon. The Corsican leader pushed far beyond the Elbe, advancing through the Netherlands and reaching the Baltic Sea. Bremen, Hamburg, and Lübeck were transformed into French-controlled port cities.

To the south, France had annexed half of Italy. By 1812, Napoleon forced both Prussia and Austria into an alliance with France, leaving Russia and Great Britain as nearly the only European powers that had not yet fallen under his domination.

their secession from the Holy Roman Empire and formed the Confederation of the Rhine under French protection, uniting sixteen German princes. Austria relinquished the German imperial title, marking the end of the empire.

Prussia's Collapse

Now only Prussia remained. In the struggle between France and the empire, Prussia, failing to understand its broader responsibility to the German people, had maintained strict neutrality and isolated itself. The French emperor seized the initiative. When it suited his purposes, Napoleon launched an offensive against Prussia.[105]

On the battlefields of Jena and Auerstedt, the once-proud army of Frederick the Great was shattered, dragging the entire Prussian kingdom into a deep decline. In the Treaties of Tilsit, Prussia was stripped of its territory up to the Elbe, with French garrisons occupying its fortresses.

Effectively, Prussia became little more than a French province, where any stirrings of national sentiment could be swiftly suppressed by the occupying forces. With this defeat, Germany as a significant political entity vanished from the map of Europe.

There was still an Austrian state, the roots and origins of which were undeniably German; however, this state had been almost entirely pushed out of Germany. Its population, apart from the core of ethnic Germans, was largely comprised of Slavs, Magyars, and Italians.[106] Its interests lay everywhere but Germany. There were many small German states, but they were French vassals bound to provide troops and pay tribute. France effectively extended as far as the Elbe. (See Map 15.)

Was there still any hope for a future?

The German People Resist Foreign Domination

---

[105] While Prussia did maintain neutrality until late 1806 and Napoleon did launch the first offensive, Prussia broke its neutrality and declared war on France first, which then prompted Napoleon to attack Prussia.

[106] Magyars are ethnic Hungarians.

Beginning in the mid-eighteenth century, the German spirit experienced a remarkable resurgence, culminating in a golden age that lasted until the mid-nineteenth century. National pride and identity began to emerge, especially within literature. This cultural awakening served as both a substitute for the lack of political unity and a forerunner to eventual national unification. In Klopstock's odes, the virtue of selfless and devoted love for the fatherland was celebrated for the first time in centuries.[107] It was an era defined by names such as Kant, Goethe, Schiller, and Lessing, names that proclaim the dominance of German thought in Europe.[108] This revival of the German spirit came about in a conscious and fervent rebellion against the tyranny of French influence, which had held Germany captive for far too long.

What unfolded in the realm of thought, literature, and philosophy found its counterpart in the fine arts, particularly in music, which more than anything else reflects the emotional life of a people. Nowhere was this more evident than in Germany, where Italian music had long held sway.

German Music Rises to the Top

In the latter half of the eighteenth century, the successful effort to break free from this foreign influence began to take shape—a drive to let the German spirit speak through music and to create an authentic expression of German sentiment. This "German music" quickly flourished, achieving remarkable mastery and earning international renown. Mozart, Gluck, Haydn, Beethoven,

---

[107] Friedrich Gottlieb Klopstock was a German poet whose odes, marked by their emotional intensity and patriotic themes, were influential in shaping the German literary movement and fostering a sense of national identity.

[108] Immanuel Kant, Johann Wolfgang von Goethe, Friedrich von Schiller and Gotthold Ephraim Lessing were pivotal figures of the German Enlightenment and classical period, with Kant revolutionizing philosophy, Goethe and Schiller elevating German literature and drama, and Lessing advancing critical thought and modern theater.

Schiller and Goethe, heralds of the German spirit

and the many who followed them soon demonstrated that Germans had taken the lead in the art of music.[109]

Yearning for a German State

One aspect deeply moves us as we reflect today on this golden age of German culture. In their thinking, poetry, and music, the nation stood united as never before. Despite their regional and religious differences, there were no divisions—only Germans.

But tragically, this industrious, self-assured, united people lacked the external framework of existence. National unity in spirit was there, but the nation-state remained a fervent hope. In the absence of such a state, one that could encompass the entire nation and command respect from the world, Frederick the Great had offered a substitute. Through his deeds and his very persona,

---

[109] Wolfgang Amadeus Mozart, Christoph Willibald Gluck, Franz Joseph Haydn and Ludwig van Beethoven were distinguished composers of the classical period.

he more than anyone else had awakened and nurtured national pride. In doing so, he had also greatly advanced literature, for in him the nation found what every people needs in order to create with joy: a hero.

Germans Flock to Prussia

A healthy and natural sense of connection to one's fatherland and people, a deep love for one's own history, and a longing for a unified state began to surface in many great figures of this era. It is no coincidence that, among the leading personalities in Prussia, we find so many names who originally came from elsewhere.

Stein, Blücher, Scharnhorst, and Gneisenau were "foreigners" in Prussia, meaning they hailed from other German states that maintained their own political independence.[110] They entered Prussian service because they recognized this state as being the key to Germany's future, and they remained loyal even after the devastating collapse of 1806. Alongside figures like Fichte, Jahn, and Arndt, they rallied the German people into a war of national liberation that, in 1813, shattered the French chains binding Germany's armies. For the old Prussia, this campaign stands as its greatest achievement, both within Germany and for Germany.

Wars of Liberation

This Prussian struggle for freedom had already taken on significance for all of Germany, as was evident in the broader German intellectual movement that fueled the war. This spirit

---

[110] Baron vom Stein, Gebhard Leberecht von Blücher, Gerhard von Scharnhorst and August Neidhardt von Gneisenau were key German leaders who opposed French influence in Prussia. Stein implemented sweeping reforms, Blücher led Prussian forces to victory against Napoleon at Waterloo, and Scharnhorst and Gneisenau reorganized the Prussian military.

found expression in the patriotic songs of Theodor Körner and Ernst Moritz Arndt, in Fichte's galvanizing speeches, and in the inspiring efforts of "Turnvater" Jahn.[111]

The Wars of Liberation did not bring Germany what its patriots had hoped for. Their longing was for a new German Reich—one that would inherit the greatness, splendor, and power of the old, with none of its flaws. They envisioned a state with secure, strong borders, unified under decisive, robust leadership. None of this became a reality. Reactionary forces, embodied by the principalities and powers at the Congress of Vienna, resisted the people's vision, and deprived them of the rewards they had so deeply hoped for from the Wars of Liberation.[112]

The self-serving ambitions of the individual German princes

"Turnvater" Jahn, Stein, and Blücher. Three champions of Germany's freedom and unity

---

[111] Friedrich Ludwig Jahn was often called "Turnvater Jahn," as he is the father of the German gymnastics movement whose members were called Turners.

[112] The Congress of Vienna was a diplomatic conference held after the Napoleonic Wars, convened from 1814 to 1815 to redraw borders and reinstate monarchies.

were further encouraged by foreign powers that had a vested interest in ensuring Germany remained fragmented and devoid of a strong central power.

Congress of Vienna

The so-called German Confederation, established at the Congress of Vienna in 1815 and comprising thirty-nine states including Austria and Prussia, was anything but a solution to the German question.[113] Instead, it only served to accentuate the damaging polarity between Prussia and Austria, which had long hindered the realization of a unified Reich. The interests of Austria and Prussia, particularly concerning Germany and the Confederation, were fundamentally at odds. Austria's priorities lay beyond Germany—in Italy, Galicia, the Balkans, and along the Adriatic Sea. To focus on German affairs would have required Austria to disregard its own concerns.

Prussia, on the other hand, had no significant interests outside Germany. All major German interests were inherently aligned with its own. This made it clear that the advancement of a unified German Reich would only come from Prussia.

Germany's Inner Turmoil

The period following the Wars of Liberation is a somber chapter in our history. It was widely understood that the prevailing state of economic disunity, with its countless customs barriers and a large multitude of insignificant states, could not continue. The foreign threats stemming from the weakness of the German Confederation's defenses were looming and could no longer be ignored. Moreover, the daily disruption to customary trade and

---

113 The German Confederation was a loose association of German states established by the Congress of Vienna to replace the Holy Roman Empire, intended to maintain regional stability and independence while balancing the influence of Austria and Prussia.

transport within the Confederation made the absurdity of this disunity all the more evident.

This fragmentation and division reduced Germany to a land ripe for exploitation by the dominant economic powers of Europe, particularly the British Empire. Achieving economic integration became as vital to national self-preservation as establishing a unified military. However, this fractured state of affairs could not be resolved with discussions alone. Carl von Clausewitz captured the sentiment of many—a vision that Otto von Bismarck would later bring to fruition:[114] "Germany can achieve political unity only by one means: the sword. This will only happen when one of its states subjugates all the others."[115]

It was clear that this state could only be Prussia, given its entire political trajectory. As a major power, Prussia was faced with a stark choice: either strive to become the leader and ruler of part (and eventually all) of Germany, or else cease to exist altogether. The legacy of Frederick the Great, disrupted by Napoleon and then restored through the Wars of Liberation, had to be brought to completion or face a second downfall. This time, such a collapse would likely be forever, taking Germany down with it.

Prussia Brings Economic Integration to Germany

In 1833, under Prussia's leadership and despite obstinate resistance, Germany was finally integrated economically. With the notable exception of the British-controlled city of Hanover

---

[114] Carl von Clausewitz was a Prussian general and military theorist best known for his seminal work *On War*, which profoundly influenced modern military strategy and introduced the concept of war as a continuation of politics by other means. Otto von Bismarck was a Prussian statesman who oversaw the eventual unification of Germany.

[115] As quoted by Hans Rothfels, *Carl von Clausewitz: Politische Schriften und Briefe* ["Carl von Clausewitz: Political Writings and Letters"], p. 171 (Munich: Drei Masken Verlag, 1922).

and the three Hanseatic cities dependent on Great Britain, all of Germany came together to form an economic coalition with unified trade policies through the *Zollverein* (the German Customs Union).[116] This union created the conditions necessary for leveraging new technological advancements in transport and commerce, such as the rise of steam engines and railroads.

The impact of this step was immediate: The yoke of foreign dominance over the German economy was lifted, enabling a united German market, under Prussia's leadership, to compete effectively on the global stage.

Attempts at Unification in 1848

The pressing force of reality demanded the political unification of the nation, but such unity could not emerge on its own. The efforts of the German bourgeoisie in 1848, culminating in the Frankfurt National Assembly, were unable to establish the German Reich, despite their good intentions.[117] The German people, caught between vague and misunderstood notions of freedom and democracy, found themselves leaderless and cast adrift, stumbling toward an uncertain future.

The time was not yet ripe for a new Reich; it was much like the insurmountable opposition Adolf Hitler faced in 1923 from a crumbling state. Prussia, once the beacon of hope for Germany, was humiliated and suppressed by the old power of Austria (that is, the Habsburgs), which had aligned itself with the interests of the international forces of Jewry, Freemasonry, and the Catholic Church. Yet, quietly, a new Germany began to

---

116 Those three Hanseatic cities were Lübeck, Bremen and Hamburg; all three would eventually accede to the union.

117 The Frankfurt National Assembly was the first parliament representing all of Germany, convened during a revolutionary wave throughout Europe to draft a constitution for a unified and democratic German state, although it ultimately failed as a result of internal divisions and lack of support from the German monarchies.

emerge, taking its initial shape under Bismarck and ultimately finding its definitive form under Hitler.

Fighting on the barricades during the revolutions of 1848

CHAPTER FIVE: THE SECOND REICH

Bismarck's Confederation

Prussia's immortal achievement lies in its determination to forge German unity, under Bismarck's leadership, with blood and iron.[118] What countless parliamentary debates, noble writings, and earnest proposals by high-minded men could not accomplish was achieved by Bismarck, a man whom our Führer has called the greatest German of modern times. In 1864, he resolved the Schleswig-Holstein question the Prussian way by reclaiming the German territory of Schleswig-Holstein in the war against Denmark.[119]

Confrontation With Austria

Bismarck quickly moved to address the most critical issue for German unification: determining leadership within the German

---

[118] "Blood and iron" refers to Bismarck's 1862 speech emphasizing the importance of military strength and decisive action, rather than diplomacy and debate, in achieving German unification under Prussian leadership.

[119] The Schleswig-Holstein question was a geopolitical dispute over the sovereignty of the duchies of Schleswig and Holstein, involving Denmark, Germany and Austria; it ultimately contributed to the rise of Prussia as a dominant power in the region following the Second Schleswig War in 1864.

Bismarck, the man who forged the Reich

realm between Prussia and Austria. Tragically, fraternal blood had to be spilled once more. The House of Habsburg, burdened with a long history of misdeeds against Germany, remained incapable of fulfilling the German longing for unity, as it increasingly grew apart from the German sphere. In 1866, at the Battle of Königgrätz, Prussia delivered the final blow to this rivalry, burying it once and for all.[120]

---

[120] The Battle of Königgrätz, the decisive conflict of the Austro-Prussian War, marked Prussia's victory over Austria, securing Prussian dominance in Germany and paving the way for German unification.

Bismarck stood entirely alone with his bold plans. It was only after the game was won that people began to grasp what had transpired over the past four years and recognize that the monumental task assigned by history to the Prussian state and the German nation had been accomplished. Austria exited the German political sphere, and with the establishment of the North German Confederation—bolstered by alliances with the Southern German states—a newly expanded Prussia took up the mantle of leadership.[121] The establishment of a unified German Reich, encompassing all of Germany, was now merely a matter of time.

The great statesman still had to avoid and delay any confrontation with France over control of the Rhine, which had been France's long-standing objective for centuries, until the victory at Königgrätz had fully solidified its political impact within Germany itself.

Germany's United Struggle Against France

Through Bismarck's masterful diplomacy, the states that had been adversaries just yesterday were transformed into allies, so that by 1870 all of Germany stood united against Napoleon III, who had watched Germany's unification first with suspicion and then with envy and resentment, much like his famous predecessor.[122] Even with France, the reckoning for past grievances had to be settled in blood.

Establishment of the German Empire

A brief war, marked by a series of brilliant military victories that vividly demonstrated Germany's superiority, wiped away the

---

121 The North German Confederation was a federal state led by Prussia that unified twenty-two Northern German states under a single constitution, serving as a precursor to the German Empire.

122 Napoleon III opposed German unification efforts, like his uncle Napoleon Bonaparte who had used the Confederation of the Rhine as an obstacle to German nationalist aspirations.

Map 16: The Reich under Bismarck in 1871

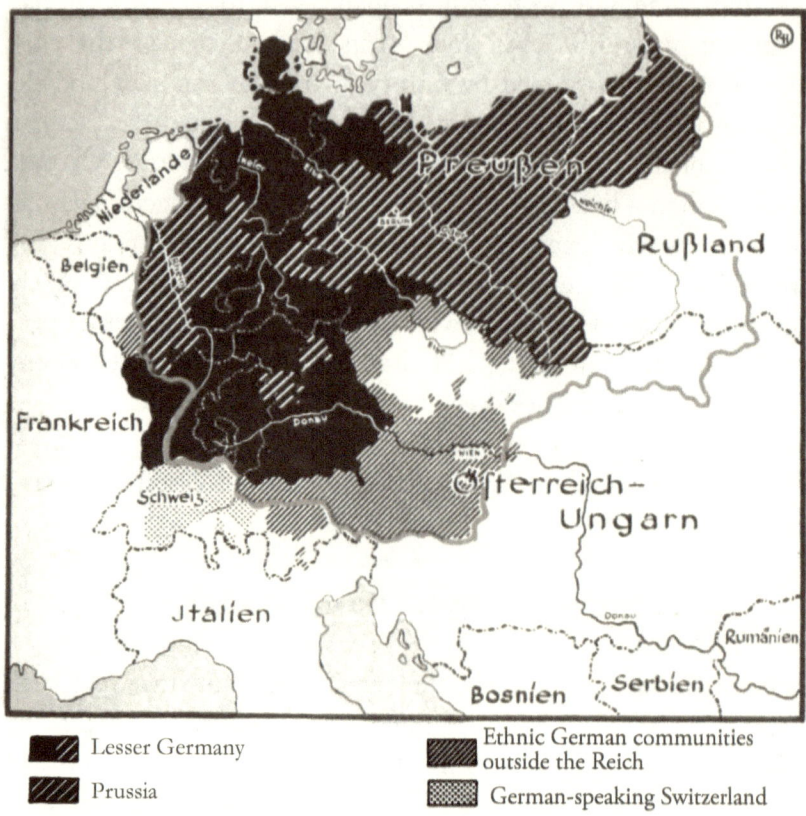

▨ Lesser Germany	▨ Ethnic German communities outside the Reich
▨ Prussia	▨ German-speaking Switzerland

Bismarck forged the Reich with blood and iron. First, Prussia addressed Germany's economic fragmentation by establishing the Zollverein in 1833, which included most Central and Southern German states—but not Austria. In the Austro-Prussian War of 1866, Bismarck removed Austria from the path toward unification, founding the North German Confederation under Prussia's leadership. The Franco-Prussian War of 1870 gave rise to the new German Empire, although, regrettably, it did not include the Germans of Austria. Thus, Bismarck's creation was not yet a nation-state, but merely an empire.

grievances of centuries. Out of this triumph, almost naturally, arose a German Reich, forged through the voluntary unification of German states. On January 18th, 1871, the German Empire was proclaimed.

Only those behind the scenes knew how much patience and diplomatic finesse had been required to secure even this final achievement. The "Lesser" German Empire was born—a federal state but not yet a true national unity.[123] The lost brother of the east, Austria, was still missing. (See Map 16.)

Foreign Envy

At the time, the world grasped the significance of this unification more clearly than the German people themselves. The established European powers felt singularly threatened. Until then, they had been able to settle their disputes on German soil, with German soldiers as their pawns. Now, however, a true great power had arisen in place of the many tiny states that had previously been so easily played off against one another. This new power seemed poised to influence all European affairs, jeopardizing the "European balance of power" that had been artificially manufactured at the Congress of Vienna in 1815 and maintained through coercion.

Germany's Economic Upturn

Economic Boom

Outwardly, the burgeoning power of the newly established Reich was first reflected in an extraordinary economic boom that spanned nearly all sectors of trade and industry. Despite occasional crises, national wealth grew steadily. Social regulations ensured the welfare of individual citizens, while the population grew strongly, which helped sustain the driving force behind Germany's continued development.

---

[123] The concept of Lesser Germany was a geopolitical solution to the German question that would unite Germany without Austria in the newly unified state. This contrasts with the concept of Greater Germany, which sought to include Austria and all German-speaking territories in a single state.

Dangers of Industrialization

Rapid industrialization, however, brought with it a dangerous shift in the balance of the nation's strength. Urban centers swelled with people, while rural areas were left desolate. Peasants not only earned less, but were often displaced from their land by foreign large-scale landholders, aided by Jewish moneylenders and merchants. This undermined the very roots of the German people. Although the nation still stood strong like a tree in the full bloom of spring, the German people focused too much on the advancements of technology and industry, forgetting that the inexhaustible wellspring of life lay in their agrarian roots.[124] The extent of the Industrial Revolution and its consequences was starkly revealed by the turn of the century, exemplified by the economic crisis of 1900, which left Germany with "only" half a million unemployed.

The crisis completely unmasked the perilous nature of unchecked capitalism, which is motivated solely by self-interest. Marxist agitators exploited this situation by promoting class struggle, a deceitful manipulation of the prevailing conditions. The worker was reduced to a "proletarian," and the peasant became the object of widespread contempt.

---

[124] National Socialist agrarian theory and policy advocated for a societal structure where the peasantry is seen as the cultural and racial foundation of the German nation, for which rural life and agricultural labor were considered essential. For further exploration of this concept, please refer to the works of R. Walther Darré, especially *Das Bauerntum als Lebensquell der nordischen Rasse* ["The Peasantry as the Lifeblood of the Nordic Race"] (Munich: J. F. Lehmanns Verlag, 1928) and *A New Nobility of Blood and Soil* [translated by Augusto Salan and Julius Sylvester] (Green Lane: Antelope Hill Publishing, 2021).

Transnational Forces

Jewry and Freemasonry

The transnational forces of Jewry and Freemasonry revealed a particularly uncompromising hostility toward a strong Germany during this period—an enmity we now recognize more clearly today, despite the skillful disguises of their attacks at the time. The nineteenth century, with its flourishing liberalism that championed untrammeled individual freedom, provided them with every opportunity to carry out their plans to undermine the nation. In just a few decades, the Jew managed to monopolize many modern tools for manipulating the state (the press, literature, art of all forms, and so forth), using financial means in an irrepressible quest for power.

The international Jew, fully aware of the stakes, understood that his final victory hinged on eradicating the racial heritage of the German people. Only then could the vision of a pan-European system under Jewish control be brought to fruition, a vision founded upon a melting pot of peoples in which Germany's distinctly Nordic racial elements would be thoroughly smothered. In this endeavor, Freemasonry served as his covert army.

The extent to which these forces brought Germany to the brink of collapse became painfully clear in the post-war years leading up to the Führer's rise to power. Yet it was precisely in that era of transformation that Germany most needed its internal strength and unity to confidently confront the foreign threats it faced.

Foreign Threats

Bismarck's Policy Toward France

France refused to understand Germany. No matter which century one examines, it is clear that France consistently worked against Germany. To put an end to this toxic relationship, Bismarck adopted a bold new policy. He sought to redirect France's energies toward pursuits outside of Europe while simultaneously preventing it from finding allies on the continent for its plans of revenge. Bismarck hoped that this approach might gradually reconcile France to the existence of a free and united Germany, thereby shielding the German people from the persistent French threat.

Although this effort ultimately failed, it does not detract from the merit of Bismarck's singular attempt to establish a genuine peace. Rather, France's relentless opposition marks it as the principal culprit behind the outbreak of the Great War.

Bismarck's Policy of Alliance

Reflecting on his time as chancellor, Bismarck later described it as dominated by one overriding concern: the fear of hostile coalitions. To prevent any military entanglements, he carefully cultivated a system of alliances. Starting in 1879, the Dual Alliance with Austria-Hungary was established, which expanded into the Triple Alliance in 1882 with the inclusion of Italy. Additionally, the League of the Three Emperors (initially formed in 1873 between Emperor William I of Germany, Emperor Franz Joseph I of Austria, and Emperor Alexander II of Russia) was renewed in 1881 and extended for another three years in 1884.[125]

Bismarck understood that these alliances were unlikely to yield substantial material advantages. However, they served the critical purpose of preventing France from forging alliances with any of these powers. At the same time, the British showed little

---

[125] These were a series of military alliances that Bismarck had pursued with the goal of maintaining peace in Europe, designed to prevent any regional superpowers from combining forces against the German Empire.

interest in becoming involved in continental disputes, as they were focused on administering their global empire.

Russia

Bismarck took particular care to ensure that the "hotline to Russia" remained intact. He never harbored any illusions about receiving direct support from Saint Petersburg, but the mutual understanding served to prevent France from aligning itself with Russia in Germany's place, which would have put Germany in a precarious position.

His Successors' Failures

Bismarck's successors found his intricate diplomacy too complex to manage. Instead of simplifying it, they clumsily dismantled it. In doing so, they alienated Russia so much that it swiftly formed a military alliance with France. Additionally, in 1895, the British and Russian empires reached an understanding through the Pamir Boundary Commission protocols regarding their spheres of influence in Central Asia. This agreement brought Russia into direct conflict with the German Empire over the issue of the Berlin–Baghdad railway.[126] Furthermore, Berlin's decision to grant Austria-Hungary a free hand in its Balkan policy only deepened the rift with Saint Petersburg.

The British Empire

France and Russia by themselves were not strong enough to challenge Germany, so they sought to involve a third power in their schemes: the British Empire. At first, Great Britain remained

---

[126] The Berlin–Baghdad railway, an ambitious project initiated by Germany to connect Europe with the Ottoman Empire, strained relations with the Russian Empire by threatening its influence in the Balkans and its access to strategic waterways.

in its "splendid isolation," focusing primarily on the expansion of its global empire.[127] Owing to its long-standing stability, the British government had overcome the internal turmoil that once posed grave threats to its existence. Both France and Russia had long stood in the way of the British Empire's ambitions in Asia and Africa. Nevertheless, Great Britain's full animosity turned against the German Empire when, in the 1880s, Germany sought to establish colonies and provide protection to its citizens worldwide through a powerful navy.

Colonies

Germany's distance from the open seas, its political weakness, economic decline and paralysis following the Thirty Years' War had long prevented it from participating in Europe's colonial ambitions. However, as German merchants began to gain influence in global trade, they found themselves subject to the whims and harassment of European rivals, not only in colonial territories but also in lands that had yet to be divided among the great powers. By the time Germany had completed its colonial acquisitions in 1885, it became clear that maintaining these possessions required the support of a strong navy. Without such protection, Germany risked building its colonial empire in vain and squandering its resources. (See Map 17.)

Great Britain Feels Threatened

Great Britain saw its global dominance, which was secured by its navy, as being under threat. It began seeking reliable allies everywhere, returning to its well-tried strategy of recruiting a "continental sword" to wield on its behalf. In the past, this role

---

[127] "Splendid isolation" refers to Great Britain's nineteenth-century diplomatic practice of avoiding permanent alliances while relying on its naval supremacy and economic power to maintain security and influence, particularly in Europe.

Map 17: Germany's Colonies until 1918

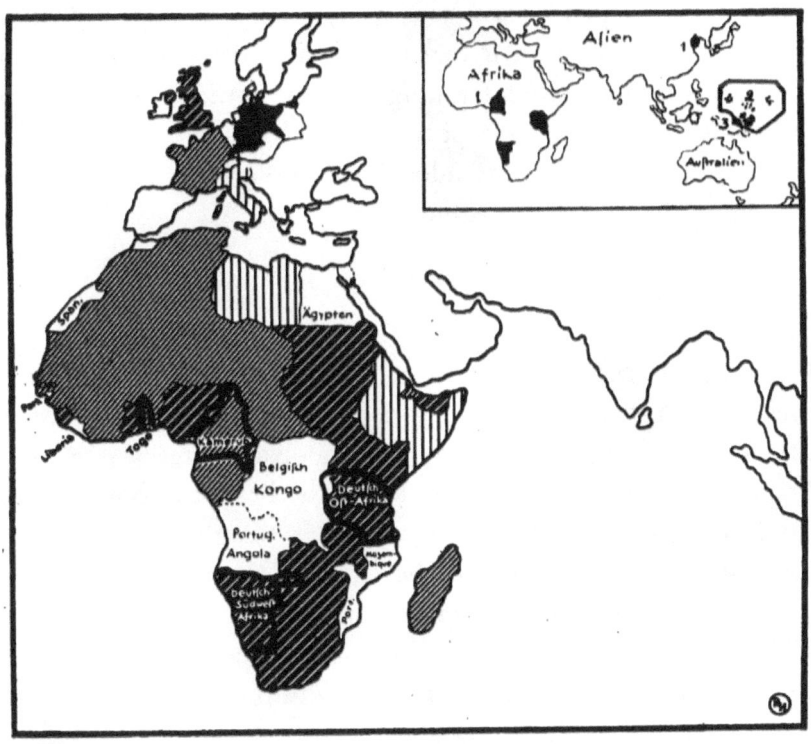

▨ British colonies	1. Kiautschou Bay
▨ French colonies	2. } German New Guinea
⫿ Italian colonies	3. }

The Treaty of Versailles stripped Germany of all its colonial possessions, depriving it of critical sources of raw materials, even though Great Britain and France, the main exploiters of those regions, already controlled vast colonial empires far larger than their populations needed. The intention was clear: to ensure that Germany remained politically and economically powerless.

had often fallen to Prussia. However, England's age-old principle of never allying with the strongest power, but rather opposing it, now prevented this approach.

Great Britain's interests have always been, and remain,

unequivocally tied to maintaining its global empire. This brand of imperialism, shaped by centuries of experience, consistently views the world from an insular perspective. The state-centric egotism reflected in this approach has long been the cornerstone of British statecraft. While this perspective may have led to a certain narrow-mindedness, it has undoubtedly also given British policy a firm and principled foundation.

A Place in the Sun

Germany, in contrast, had to rely on a "system of makeshift measures" in its political strategy to carve out its rightful place in the sun amid the firmly entrenched global interests of Russia, France, and Great Britain.[128] It lacked the benefit of both a solid tradition and any significant experience in this realm. As a result, Germany was never afforded the strategic freedom necessary to pursue a coherent and principled approach to foreign policy.

Under the pressure of these circumstances, Germany occasionally substituted its policy of an open hand with that of a clenched fist, yet it refrained from stepping outside the fragile framework of diplomacy or endangering European peace with threats of war. Germany remained fully aware of its responsibility within Europe.

Subversion of the Empire From Within

Subversion from within the empire increased at an alarming pace. Opposing forces—including liberalism and democracy, particularism, the political influence of the Church, and the overt

---

[128] The phrase "system of makeshift measures" is attributable to Helmuth von Moltke the Elder in his essay *Über Strategie* (1871), found in *Moltkes militärische Werke* ["Moltke's Military Works"], vol. 2, part 2, p. 293 (Berlin: E. S. Mittler und Sohn, 1900). The famous statement typified his belief that no simple rules or formulas existed for determining military plans.

hostility of the Social Democrats toward the empire—were still kept in check by Bismarck's strong personality.[129] However, these tensions portended a looming catastrophe.

The German Army

The only visible embodiment of national unity during this period was the German army, whose role as an unparalleled institution for the education and discipline of the German people cannot be overstated. Adolf Hitler articulated this in *Mein Kampf* with the following words:

> The army stood as the greatest asset during this initial era of the slowly advancing disintegration of our national body. It was the most formidable school of the German nation, and it is no coincidence that the hatred of all our enemies was directed against this bulwark of national self-preservation and freedom. ... What the German people owe to the army can be summed up in a single word: Everything.
>
> The army instilled a sense of absolute responsibility at a time when this quality had become increasingly rare, when shirking responsibility was becoming commonplace and encouraged by the epitome of irresponsibility itself, that is, the parliament. The army cultivated personal courage in the people at a time when cowardice was threatening to become an epidemic. The spirit of self-sacrifice for the common good was often dismissed as foolishness, while those deemed wise were the ones most adept at protecting and promoting their

---

[129] Owing to its Marxist ideology, the Social Democratic Party of Germany (SPD) was ideologically opposed to much of Bismarck's policies and was for over a decade outlawed for its revolutionary, anti-monarchist sentiments. It was a Social Democrat who "proclaimed" the end of the German Empire and the birth of the Weimar Republic. Many of its more radical members would split from the SPD to form an even more revolutionary party that fomented a number of local insurrections throughout Germany toward the end of the First World War.

own interests. The army served as the school that taught individual Germans to seek the salvation of their nation not in the hollow phrases of international brotherhood between Africans, Germans, Chinese, French or English, but in the strength and determination of their own people.

The army taught resolve to the people at a time when indecision and doubt were beginning to dominate their actions in life. It meant something, at a time when troublemakers had the greatest say in everything, to uphold the principle that any command is better than none at all. . . . The army instilled idealism and devotion to the fatherland in its soldiers, while materialism and greed were spreading unchecked elsewhere. It united the people as one, countering class division.

The greatest accomplishment of the army of the bygone German Empire lies in its ability, at a time of mass conformity and no individuality, to value individuals above the masses. In opposition to the Judeo-democratic notion of blind worship of the majority, the army defended its belief in the value of personality. This enabled the army to foster what was needed most at the time: Men of character.

What many Germans, whether blinded by ignorance or driven by ill will, refused to recognize was clear to the rest of the world: The German army was the greatest weapon in the service of the German nation's freedom and the sustenance of its children. [130]

How desperately Germany needed this institution became apparent in the colossal struggle of nations that began in 1914.

---

[130] *Mein Kampf,* vol. I, chapter 10.

Germany's Political Decline

The economic rise of the German people masked their political decline. The German nation believed it could rest complacently on the laurels of its victory in the Franco-Prussian War, yet what had been achieved through blood and iron, through the collective will of the German spirit, could only be preserved if the people united in lasting solidarity. The division into classes based on material wealth or social status—deliberately stirred up by international capital and world Jewry—proved fatal at the critical hour, when the nation required the ultimate dedication of its strength to preserve its German identity.

The imperial government, lacking true leadership, remained blind to the spiritual malaise of the German people, rendering it powerless and defenseless. The Wilhelmine era resulted in an intellectual stagnation and a descent into a bleak materialism across all domains, which became the most telling symptom of the racial decline of the German people.[131]

Value of Race

Disregard for our own race and its inherent value, as well as the contempt for the destiny and responsibility bestowed upon us, represents the greatest sin committed by the German people of that era, seduced by the illusion of economic prosperity. As a nation, we had not yet cultivated the character needed to become a truly exemplary people in the highest sense. Once more, fate inexorably subjected us to its harsh lessons, only enabling us to rediscover our German nature and embrace our purpose in the world under Hitler's leadership.

---

[131] The Wilhelmine era refers to the period of German history from approximately 1888 to 1918, during the reign of Emperor Wilhelm II, marked by aggressive industrialization, imperial expansion and growing militarism, which contributed to the tensions leading to the First World War.

Germany's Hour of Isolation[132]

The policy of isolation that ultimately led to the empire being encircled by a ring of hostile nations at the outbreak of the Great War could have been avoided with a measure of prudence on the part of German statesmen.[133] The inadequate efforts of German diplomacy to extricate itself from this predicament marked the beginning of the Wilhelmine era in foreign policy.

The first mistake was the failure to renew the Reinsurance Treaty with the Russian Empire, despite Russia's pleas for its continuation.[134] The foreign policy implications were immediate: Germany was now left to rely solely on the Triple Alliance with Austria-Hungary and Italy. This shift transformed Austria-Hungary's dependency on the German Empire into a German reliance on Austria-Hungary, binding the empire to the Habsburg monarchy in a union of life or death. Unfortunately, this alliance tethered Germany to a state whose internal stability was already in serious doubt as a result of persistent national conflicts.

On the other hand, this move released France from its most dangerous adversary, opening the door for a rapprochement between France and Russia. The milestones of this development, which we can clearly trace today, included the Franco-Russian Alliance of 1891, which was soon fortified by a military convention the following year and then a naval convention in 1912. The barrier between autocratic

---

[132] "Hour of isolation" is a paraphrase of an extract from Ernst Bassermann's speech to the German Reichstag, dated November 14th, 1906, in which Bassermann claimed Germany's hour of isolation is impending.

[133] The policy of isolation refers to the German Empire's perception during the late nineteenth and early twentieth centuries that it was being diplomatically isolated and surrounded by hostile powers, particularly France, Great Britain and Russia, through alliances and agreements aimed at containing its influence.

[134] The Reinsurance Treaty was a secret agreement between Germany and Russia, orchestrated by Bismarck, to ensure mutual neutrality in the event of a war with a third party, aiming to prevent Germany's diplomatic isolation while balancing alliances in Europe.

1914 to 1918

The German Reichstag on July 19th, 1917, following the introduction of the Peace Resolution by the Jewish traitor Oskar Cohn

Soldiers fight while politicians talk!

Russia and democratic France had been dismantled.

France's efforts to win British friendship eventually bore fruit. The signing of the Entente Cordiale in 1904, the "cordial agreement," resolved the colonial disputes between the two powers, clearing the way for cooperative engagement in European affairs as well.[135] Remarkably, a reconciliation between even Great Britain and Russia was achieved in 1907, despite previous significant tensions between the two. These included sharp rivalries in Central and South Asia, where they had once stood as adversaries.[136]

This effectively marked the formation of the Triple Entente between France, Russia, and Great Britain. The United Kingdom further solidified its diplomatic strategy by mediating a settlement between Russia and Japan, thereby eliminating another potential source of conflict.

---

[135] The Entente Cordiale was a series of agreements between the United Kingdom and France that signified the beginning of their cooperation against German ambitions in Europe.

[136] The Anglo-Russian Convention of 1907 was an agreement between the United Kingdom and Russia that ended their rivalry in Asia, known as the Great Game, by delineating their spheres of influence primarily in Persia, Afghanistan and Tibet.

Russia, having shifted its focus from Asia back to the Ottoman Empire and its ambitions in the Balkans, inevitably exacerbated tensions with Austria-Hungary; because of its alliance with the Dual Monarchy, Germany also became more entangled in these Balkan conflicts.[137] Russia advanced its Balkan policy in a deliberate scheme, pursuing its interests at the expense of Austria-Hungary. A key success of Russian diplomacy was the formation of the Balkan League in 1912, aimed squarely against the Ottoman Empire.

France's primary focus now turned to winning over Italy, which found its expansive ambitions constrained by the purely defensive nature of the Triple Alliance. Italy's broader goals could only be achieved with British cooperation. At the same time, France was more willing than ever to make concessions to secure Italy's allegiance. This led to an agreement between France and Italy regarding the Mediterranean in 1902.[138]

Italy's ambitions and demands were primarily territorial in nature. Its first attempt to acquire Abyssinia in 1867 ended disastrously with the crushing defeat at Adwa in 1896. Afterward, its focus shifted to other objectives: expansion into Trieste, Istria, Dalmatia, the Austrian territories, and the central Mediterranean. Achieving the first goal would come at the expense of its Austrian ally, while anything more than that could only be realized with the assistance of France and the United Kingdom.

Italy's estrangement from the Triple Alliance, which began in 1902, became increasingly apparent. The meeting between Emperor Nicholas II of Russia and King Victor Emmanuel III of Italy in 1909 further advanced this rift. During this encounter, the Russians expressed their approval of Italy's territorial

---

137 "The Dual Monarchy" is a synonym for Austria-Hungary.

138 This agreement meant that Italy would not go to war against France (and thus not support Germany against France), regardless of its membership in the Triple Alliance.

ambitions in Tripoli and Cyrenaica.[139] In return, Italy agreed to consider Russian interests in the Turkish Straits favorably, effectively aligning itself against its Austrian ally in this matter as well.[140]

By reviewing the development of the Triple Entente, which had its beginnings in 1891 and evolved into a united front against Germany by 1914, it becomes clear that the core of the Entente was the Franco-Russian Alliance, later strengthened by Great Britain's participation. Japan remained their peripheral ally, while Italy was poised to become a future accomplice in war. Russia bolstered its position through Balkan alliances, successfully bringing Romania into its sphere of influence, although Bulgaria was ultimately excluded. Following the First Balkan War, Serbia and Greece, joined by Romania and Montenegro, turned against Bulgaria, stripping it of most of its territorial gains from the Ottomans, who managed to reclaim a portion of their lost lands.

On the other side of Europe, Great Britain successfully brought Belgium into the anti-German front indirectly with conversations between the two nations in 1906. By 1908, certainly no later than 1912, the Central Powers were effectively isolated—a development for which German policy itself also bore responsibility.

Dearth of Capable Politicians

None of Bismarck's successors ever came close to matching the Iron Chancellor's achievements. If Bismarck had one

---

[139] Tripoli and Cyrenaica are the two historical provinces making up the western and eastern halves, respectively, of today's Libya.

[140] The Turkish Straits, consisting of the Bosporus and the Dardanelles, are a strategic chokepoint connecting the Black Sea to the Mediterranean. Control over the straits was a recurring geopolitical issue in the nineteenth and twentieth centuries, known as the "Straits Question," involving disputes over access and sovereignty between Russia, Austria-Hungary, the Ottoman Empire and other great powers.

Map 18: The Great Fraud of Versailles

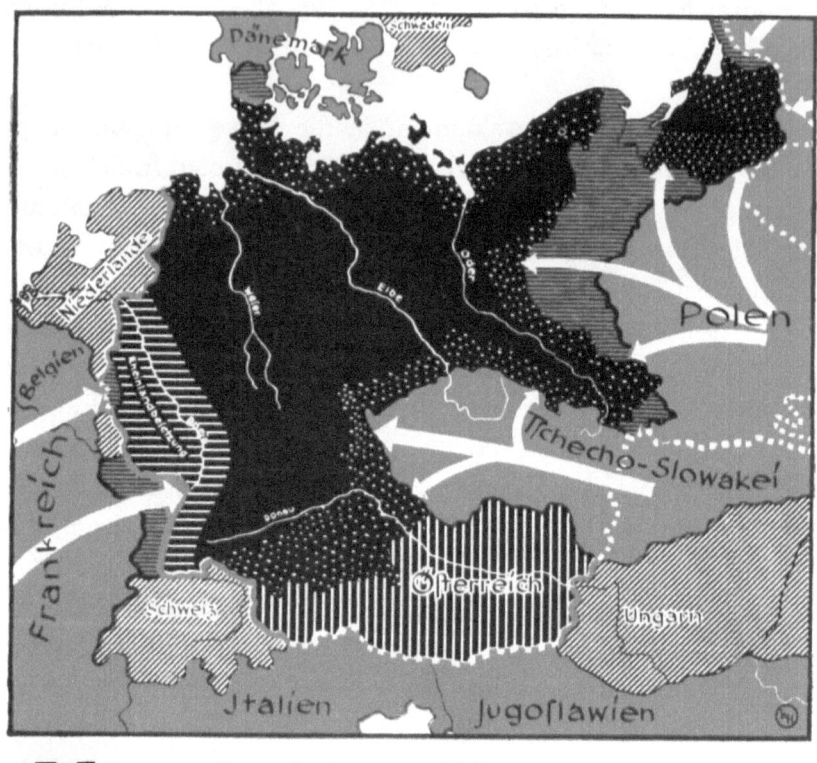

▰ Remaining German land		▥ Austria	
▰ Demilitarized Rhineland		▭ Beneficiaries of Versailles	
▰ Areas prohibited of fortification		▨ Neutral states	
▰ German losses			

Thus, in 1919, Germany was dismembered and dishonored, stripped of its rights so as to permanently subjugate it. Lands that had been part of the Reich and its destiny from time immemorial were torn away: Northern Schleswig, West Prussia, Posen, the Memel Territory, Upper Silesia, Alsace, Lorraine, Eupen and Malmedy.

On top of that, the entire western region of the now-diminished Reich was demilitarized. The entire northern coastline, nearly the entire eastern border and all of Southern Germany were prohibited from having fortifications. The Reich was dispossessed of control over its own rivers, which were "internationalized." Vast swaths of land endured years of foreign occupation. Austria was outright forbidden from uniting with the Reich.

shortcoming, it was his failure to establish a school of diplomacy capable of continuing his legacy.

Great Britain had long possessed a politically trained leadership within its aristocracy, and France within its upper bourgeoisie. In contrast, the great unified state with its grand ambitions was still too young in Germany. Its educational and cultural systems were still largely shaped by the traditions of its former fragmented states, leaving political knowledge in the nation insufficiently developed. Moreover, the civil service, by its very nature, was ill-suited to adopt a truly statesmanlike vision and remained too entrenched in outdated notions and habits to provide effective leadership.

The National Socialist state consciously sought to counter this danger. It established Adolf Hitler Schools, National Political Institutes of Education, and NS-*Ordensburgen,* where the next generation of leaders is trained.

CHAPTER SIX:
THE COMING OF THE
NSDAP

The Great War as the Seedbed of National Awakening

The Great War was merely the inevitable result of the many tensions described above. Someone once remarked that Europe "stumbled" into war in 1914. This phrase aptly captures the fateful nature of the inevitable conflict. While the United Kingdom may have sought the war and the entire policy of Edward the "Encircler" and his foreign secretary Edward Grey was directed toward delivering a crushing blow to the rising German Empire,[141] none of these warmongers could have foreseen that this war was merely the prelude to the ultimate, decisive confrontation in which we now find ourselves.

---

[141] Emperor Wilhelm II often referred to King Edward VII as an "encircler" because of his persistent efforts to contain German influence in Europe. Edward was the uncle of Wilhelm, and they had a poor personal relationship which also strained the relations between their countries. As British Foreign Secretary, Sir Edward Grey also contributed to British policy with the goal of checking Germany's growing power.

Community of all Germans

In the fateful days of August 1914, as the German people came to terms with their situation, they demonstrated their innate strength and resolve. Germans rediscovered their unity, casting aside divisions of class and social standing, and prepared to shatter the framework that had held sway for over a century. The thunder of artillery fire transformed class warriors into true soldiers, fighting for their people and fatherland. The storm of the moment swept away the fog of Marxist illusions; the creed of individualism was trampled upon by thousands of marching feet. Men who, just yesterday, held nothing more sacred than the melody of "The Internationale" today advanced against the enemy with "Das Lied der Deutschen" on their lips.[142]

For four years, the gray-clad German soldier fought with the clear understanding that the very existence of his people was at stake, and in the mud of the cratered battlefields, outdated values sank into oblivion. Shellfire tore apart an entire era of rot; what still held sway back home was irrelevant here. In the fire of this war, the people were being made ready for 1933. The lived experience of their united fighting spirit would bear fruit. The seeds were sown, and a harvest was destined to follow.

This is the law of life, which also governs the awakening of a nation. The stab in the back, and all that followed in its wake, was destined to remain barren; it could destroy, but it could not create. But the front line, which witnessed the shared struggle of an entire people, carried within it the seeds of future growth.

---

[142] "The Internationale" is a revolutionary anthem that has served as a rallying song of various far-left organizations since it was first written in 1871; in fact, a version of it would eventually become the national anthem of the Soviet Union. "Das Lied der Deutschen" is a patriotic German song and was later adopted as the national anthem of Germany in 1922.

The Great Fraud Of Versailles

Collapse of 1918

The Reich's total collapse in 1918 could only occur because an enemy within extended a hand of betrayal to the foreign adversary. Politicians failed to support military leadership; while the troops performed heroic deeds, the government and the nation's politicians offered the dismal spectacle of indecisive gridlock and constant wavering. On November 9th, 1918, the long-prepared revolution erupted. This opened the way for Germany's foreign enemies to press their boot firmly on its neck: On November 11th, the armistice came into effect, to which the military was forced to submit, as continuing the fight with revolution brewing at home seemed impossible.

From this emerged the disgraceful Treaty of Versailles, which embodied the enemy's intent to annihilate the German people by any means. Mutilated by the cession of Alsace, Lorraine, Eupen, and Malmedy in the west, as well as Pomerelia, Danzig, Posen, Upper Silesia, and Memel in the east; rendered powerless by restricting its troops to a laughably small number, demolishing its fortifications, and prohibiting the defense of its Rhine border; and burdened with crushing reparations far into the future—Germany was hurled into a deeper state of powerlessness and defenselessness than it had ever known. All the while, it remained beset by hostile neighbors to both the east and west, who made no secret of their ambitions to seize even more German territory. (See Map 18.)

CHAPTER SEVEN: THE NATIONAL SOCIALIST MOVEMENT

Years of Powerlessness, Hardship, and Disgrace

Years of powerlessness, hardship, and disgrace followed—years that remain a haunting memory for every German who lived through them. Germany was torn apart by strife between political parties, a discord fueled by foreign elements. Germans turned against one another, fighting to the delight of their enemies: Jews and Freemasons, even Englishmen and Frenchmen. The people were left destitute by the ruthless exploitation of that shameful treaty. On the international stage, Germany was stripped of its rights and its dignity, having been reduced to a mere plaything in the hands of its enemies. Such was the state of the nation.

The Struggle of the NSDAP

At that time, it required an unshakeable faith not to despair of Germany's future. By all human reckoning, there seemed little reason for hope. Even through this darkest trial in their history, however, the German people endured. In their hour of greatest need, a new Führer arose, a man who had a new vision for the nation. He transformed a mere sentiment into the clear recognition of the fact that Germany's collapse had been made possible only by the lack of alignment between its people, its leadership, and a cohesive worldview. He charted the path that pulled Germany out of the abyss.

The political rise of the Führer and his movement, the NSDAP, culminating in their assumption of power, seems to us today almost like a miracle.

Adolf Hitler As Führer

From a group of seven steadfast German men emerged a powerful figure forged in the crucible of the Great War. This man arose from the camaraderie of those who had conquered all fear of death, for death had been their constant companion through four long years of sacrifice. No one yet knew his name. Despite all the suffering that the war brought upon Germany, there remains for us some solace in its conclusion.

The fallen unknown soldier, whose heroism and greatness command the reverence of all nations, found form and new life in Germany. Two million men did not die in vain. We do not stand before the memorials of the fallen soldiers merely to lay flowers upon lifeless stone. The legacy of the unknown soldier directs our thoughts and heartfelt remembrance to the Führer of the German Reich, who was a comrade to those men in their suffering and mortal struggle, in the truest and noblest sense of the word. He is the Führer of the Reich for which they gave their young lives, and he embodies the spirit of the unknown soldier today.

Betrayal of 1923

The Führer revealed his abilities gradually over time. After the attempt to create a new Germany from Bavaria failed because of the betrayal of its leaders, he persevered, striving tirelessly to achieve

Map 19: Europe's Struggle against Bolshevism and British Imperialism

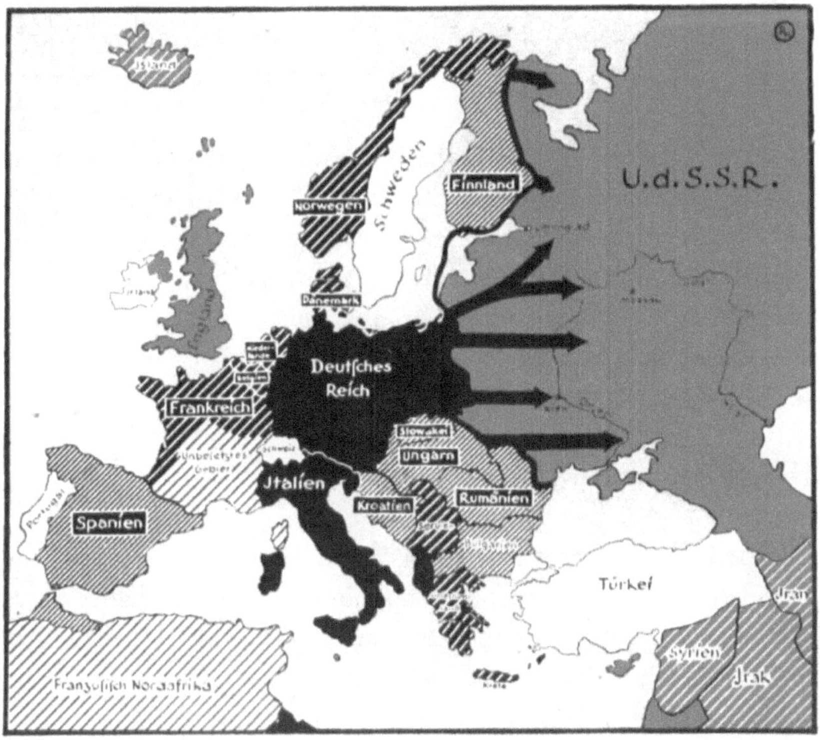

As of September 1941

▨	Territory occupied by Germany or Italy	☐	Neutral countries
▨	German-friendly	Spanien	Countries with volunteer forces against Bolshevism
▨	Enemy-occupied territory		

Under Germany's leadership, having cast off the chains of the Treaty of Versailles, Europe now stands almost entirely united in the struggle for a new and just order against those enemies who have long exploited our continent as the battleground for their self-serving and destructive ambitions.

power through lawful means.[143] Within a few short years, despite intense opposition from the parties supported by Jewry and Freemasonry, he succeeded in making the NSDAP the strongest political movement in the country. All the while, the unification of the German people into a genuine national unity was his constant focus and goal.

By the summer of 1932, the NSDAP won two hundred thirty seats in the Reichstag, while the total number of representatives from bourgeois parties dwindled to slightly over one hundred fifty. Meanwhile, communism sensed the existential threat posed by this burgeoning movement and resorted to its most brutal methods. The many bloody sacrifices made by members of the movement stand as a testament to the struggle against those subhumans.

Hitler Assumes Power

The period of greatest tension began in 1933. On January 30th, President Paul von Hindenburg appointed Hitler as Chancellor to lead the government of the German people.[144] The struggle for power had come to an end: Through lawful means, the Führer achieved victory despite the most brazen provocations.

---

[143] The Beer Hall Putsch of 1923, an attempted coup by Hitler and the NSDAP to seize power in Munich, failed after key German leaders, including Bavarian officials, withdrew their support and helped stop the coup, leading to its swift suppression.

[144] Paul von Hindenburg was a military leader and statesman who served as the President of the Weimar Republic from 1925 to 1934.

CHAPTER EIGHT: THE THIRD REICH

Victory of Nationalist Thought

What legacy did our Führer inherit? A Germany in chains, with unemployment soaring to nearly seven million, plunging the nation into unprecedented misery. Even in the face of these overwhelming challenges, the Führer never lost his unshakeable resolve and faith. Through his determination, he continually uplifted even the most despairing in his own ranks.

Leadership of the Führer

The dreadful legacy he inherited demanded extraordinary skill, nerves of steel, and a bold, clear will. With firm and decisive hands, the Führer grabbed the wheel of the state and steered the ship of Germany onto a direct and purposeful course. Peace and order returned to the nation almost immediately. Within an astonishingly short time, the corrosive poison of communism was eradicated, and the unemployment crisis was resolved within four years, as planned.[145] Germany's honor and freedom were restored, without its old foes daring to take up arms against the Führer. In March 1935, the Luftwaffe was established; in May of the same year, compulsory military service was introduced; and by March 1936, the demilitarized zone in the Rhineland was reoccupied.

Versailles in Tatters

The disgraceful Treaty of Versailles lay in tatters, its creators too afraid to act in its defense. Bold and swift decisions, as well as a sharp understanding of the inner weaknesses of our adversaries, had secured this triumph.

Beginning of a True German Reich

The resurgence of military strength soon allowed for the removal of the unnatural borders imposed in 1919. Supported by the friendship of Italy, our Führer led the annexation of Austria by the Reich in March 1938, satisfying the long-felt yearning of all Germans and healing the wound that Bismarck had once left on German hearts. In October of the same year, the Germans in Bohemia and Moravia were freed from Czech rule. This was followed by the establishment of the Protectorate, the incorporation of the General Government into the Reich, and the reintegration of the eastern provinces.[146] In short, the borders in the east and west were redefined and rectified.

---

[145] The Four Year Plan, introduced in 1936 by Hitler under Hermann Göring's leadership, was an extensive series of economic measures aimed at achieving autarky, easing unemployment, overhauling infrastructure, rearming the military and strengthening the economy through increased industrial production and self-sufficiency.

[146] The Protectorate of Bohemia and Moravia and the General Government for the Occupied Polish Region were German-occupied territories during the Second World War, while the eastern provinces were those former German lost to Poland after the First World War.

The *Reichsadler*, the symbol of the German Reich

The Current Configuration of the Reich

With recent events, the German Reich has almost entirely regained the territory it once held in ancient times. Its internal unity has been fully realized, and anything that stood in the way has been removed. What had once been only a cherished aspiration through the millennia of German history is now becoming a reality. (See Map 19.)

German Aspirations

The new Reich, the eternal Reich of the Germans, is rising!

It was the fate of the Germans that our people could never find their true form, that there was always a divide between their outer appearance and their inner essence. The people and the state seldom aligned and never fully harmonized. Such perfect harmony remained the ultimate goal, almost becoming a myth, the "myth of the Reich."

Time and again, we witness in the seemingly dry and matter-of-fact depictions of maps the unfolding of the German tragedy: the concentrated focus of all the people's strength, the great leap forward, and then, just before reaching the long-sought goal, the slipping away, the sudden fall.

The Germanic peoples have long endured this cycle of struggle and collapse; the Carolingian Empire succumbed to it, the Hohenstaufen Empire collapsed under its weight, and the Hohenzollern Empire perished before it. Now, in this historically significant era, Adolf Hitler dared to take this leap once more— and for the first time, we have witnessed success. The Reich, for which we have long yearned, has become reality: the true German Reich.

The Reich of Charlemagne transformed into the Holy Roman Empire of the German Nation under his successor, Otto I. When Bismarck re-established the Reich in 1871, it was a German nation-state, but an incomplete one. Bismarck was constrained to leave parts of the German people outside its borders, unable to pursue a broader pan-German policy without risking conflict with other powers. Austria-Hungary had to remain intact, as Germany was in desperate need of allies. Political realities imposed limits on Bismarck's ambitions.

Today, however, the Reich is truly German, politically encompassing all Germans for the first time, securing the connection between the people and the state. In the face of grave

Adolf Hitler, the Führer of the German Reich

hardship and profound humiliation, the German people have proven themselves not as slaves to their fate but as its masters. From this, the past four thousand years gain their meaning in the present and provide a guiding vision for the future.

Germans Are the Foundation of the Reich

Today, we are convinced that the current German Reich, in its fundamental structure, is the result of a long historical development ordained by Providence. Its racial basis, leadership principles, and ideological underpinnings align with our nature and are therefore correct.

The foundation of our Reich is the German people. Man is bound by divine law to his national community, for better or worse. Our state is built on this understanding—not as an end in itself but as a means to preserve, protect, and foster the growth of our people, from whom all foreign elements must be removed so as to maintain our integrity.

It was, therefore, a logical step for the Reich to enact special laws aimed at preserving and promoting a racially pure and genetically healthy population. Two such laws stand out as examples, highlighting the Führer's desire to unconditionally safeguard and nurture the hereditary and racial values of our nation while ensuring that this heritage would be protected from degenerative influences in future generations by preventing the proliferation of those who are genetically unfit.

On October 1st, 1933, the Ancestral Estate Law came into effect, aimed at securing the peasantry as the lifeblood and foundation of the German state. It was followed on January 1st, 1934, by the Law for the Prevention of Hereditarily Diseased Offspring.[147]

The idea of the people as a living organism, as a collective entity, is becoming ever clearer in the mind of every member

---

[147] The Ancestral Estate Law was legislation meant to preserve German agricultural heritage by designating certain farms as ancestral estates that could only be passed down to Aryan descendants, preventing their sale or division and ensuring rural stability in line with the NSDAP's blood and soil policy. The Law for the Prevention of Hereditarily Diseased Offspring allowed for the compulsory sterilization of individuals with certain genetic conditions, as part of the government's broader eugenics program.

of the nation. The concept of the national community serves as the starting point for all our actions.[148]

Germany and the Germanic Sphere

The Reich is already taking another step forward. The current war, which was forced upon us, has brought us a victory: the duty to protect other Germanic peoples—tribes that are either relatives of our forefathers or that belonged to the Reich for centuries, only to be separated by unfortunate developments.

Party and State

The living conscience of the people is embodied in the party. It serves as the bearer of the will of the Reich, and in it converge all the dynamic forces that, shaped by thousands of years of hard-earned experience, have now emerged. Within the state, these forces take form and direction.

The party permeates the state, which exists solely as a means to an end. The state is the concrete representation of the political and ideological will of the people. Its officials must never see themselves as mere bureaucrats or recipients of pensions, but rather as responsible soldiers with a fighting spirit and as dedicated stewards of the national community.

The state is structured according to these principles. It is a state with a leader, founded on authority that flows downward and obedience that flows upward. The principles and practices that bind the Reich together are rooted in the ancient Germanic concept of loyalty: a relationship between leaders and followers that can only exist in a community of shared blood. This bond is built on the

---

148 The "national community" in German is called the *Volksgemeinschaft*. It is a central concept in National Socialism that envisions a racially unified, classless society which prioritizes collective loyalty to the nation; it shaped the policies of the NSDAP to reorganize German society around principles of racial purity, national solidarity and shared purpose.

trust of the followers in their leaders and the respect of the leaders for their followers. In this way, the Reich becomes a true democracy, that is, a state of and for the people.

Reich Government

The Reich Government is composed of the Führer and Chancellor of Germany, along with his ministers. Each minister oversees his designated responsibilities in accordance with the directives and instructions of the Führer, who holds ultimate authority over all political and economic matters. The Führer and Chancellor serves as the head of the Reich, possessing the power to intervene in every aspect of state life. All state authorities and instruments of power are at his disposal. The objectives of the party serve as guiding principles for the state.

States

The states within the Reich have relinquished their political and governmental independence, now functioning only as administrative divisions of the Reich. Beyond this, they retain significance in terms of regional identity and cultural policy. However, in all matters, they are subordinate to the Reich. Each is overseen by a Reich Governor, who acts as a representative of the Reich. In Prussia, the Führer exercises the authority of the Reich Governor, delegating these powers to Hermann Göring as Minister President of Prussia.

Reichstag

The Reichstag is the representative body of the German people. It is convened by the President of the Reichstag as ordered by the Führer. Its primary function is to grant approval to the declarations of the Reich Government by a simple majority vote.

Restructuring the Reich

Step by step, the purposeful restructuring of the Reich was implemented via legislation: The Law to Secure the Unity of Party and State of 1933 solidified the close integration of the state and the National Socialist movement. The Law on the Reconstruction of the Reich of 1934 ended centuries of fragmentation within the German nation by abolishing the political independence of individual states, designating them administrative units. The Law on the Head of State of the German Reich of 1934 firmly established unified leadership for the people and the state. Lastly, the Decree on the Appointment of a Chief of the German Police of 1936 centralized all police responsibilities under a single command. With it, the Führer appointed *Reichsführer-ᛋᛋ* Heinrich Himmler as Chief of the German Police.

Wehrmacht

The monumental achievements of the National Socialist state, faced with a world of envious adversaries, were made possible only through the simultaneous establishment of well-organized and disciplined armed forces. This military force has already demonstrated its strength in recent times and will continue to do so. The Wehrmacht, alongside the party, constitutes the second pillar supporting the Reich. Every healthy citizen not only bears the will of his people, but must also defend his people. Together, the party and the Wehrmacht ensure the realization and enduring stability of the Reich.

The Reich and the World

The Reich's position in relation to the rest of the world is based on the natural right of a nation to claim its fair share on earth, a share warranted by its size, strength, and achievements. This ensures that

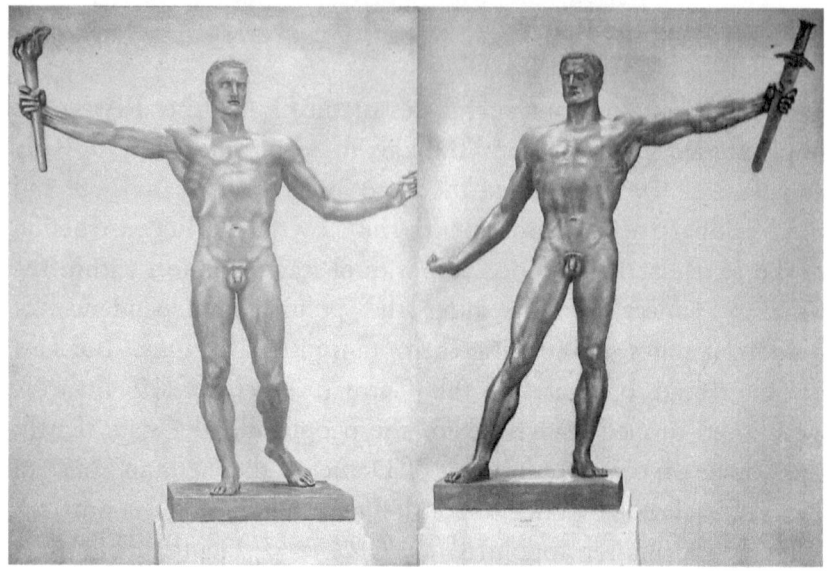

Fackelträger   *Schwertträger*

every individual within the nation is guaranteed a dignified existence.

The cooperation of all peoples of Germanic heritage is, furthermore, our natural goal. Equality among all nations on the earth, within this framework of peaceful cooperation for the benefit of our people and mankind in general, forms the foundation of our foreign policy.

Germany, the Heart of Europe

Germany has always been the heart of Europe, and the German Reich stands as the core intellect of our continent—a geopolitical outcome of a long and often painful process. The German Reich has finally become a powerful European nucleus, whose existence no longer depends on the competence or vision of individual politicians. Instead, it endures because the dynamic vitality of our people has, by absolute necessity, triumphed over lifeless philosophies.

Rome–Berlin Axis

Together with Italy, its former partner in the Holy Roman Empire during the Middle Ages (albeit under tumultuous circumstances), Germany now asserts its leadership in Europe. Political, economic and cultural power emanates from the German Reich, influencing and enriching the surrounding nations of Europe. If even the incomplete Reich of the Middle Ages, unaware of its own national

Waffen-ᛋᛋ in action

strength, was able to lead Europe, how much more fitting is it for the modern Reich and its people to assume this role? A nation that completed its historical development later than others, that endured harsher trials and underwent a longer refinement, now emerges as a youthful and powerful force at the dawn of a new era.

Germany's Claim to Leadership

Germany does not seek to establish a system of exploitative dominance, like the English plutocrats who prosper at the expense of other nations. Instead, our claim to leadership in Europe and the world is grounded in Germany's divinely ordained development as a guiding nation. It is built on achievement, merit, dedication, justice, and exemplary conduct. We see it as our mission to demonstrate once again the higher standard of German leadership, and to bring a new, fairer order to Europe.

The Mission of the SS

When we enshrine the concept of community as understood by National Socialism as the ideological foundation of the Reich, it must not remain merely a statement. A worldview that does not evolve into a set of fundamental convictions remains nothing more than empty phrases. Besides, any conviction that fails to establish a new order is meaningless and will make no mark on the world.

Likewise, we can only bring the Reich to its greatest fruition as a historic European reality if we truly find the strength to instill the worldview of National Socialism as a deep-seated conviction in all Germans. From this conviction, and upon it, we must then build the new and just order of the Reich.

It is, therefore, essential to cultivate the constructive and defensive forces within the German people for the future. The task is to awaken the Nordic heritage in those who are apathetic or unwilling to open their eyes, so that our natural worldview can flow

Original 1941 cover of *Rise of the Reich*: The eagle brooch, superimposed on the *Reichsadler*, is an *Ostrogothic* work of art from Cesena, dated approximately to the sixth century ad. It is made of gold with inlays of almandine.

anew, invigorating and permeating the collective spirit of all German people.

According to the intentions of the *Reichsführer-ᛋᛋ*, the *Schutzstaffel* is to serve not only its conventional military duties, but also to act as combat troops for the ideological goals of the new Reich.[149] Therefore, the ᛋᛋ man is a fighter equipped with both a worldview and a weapon, fully aware that the enduring security of the Reich depends fundamentally on the combination of both elements—ideology and force.

The statues *Fackelträger* and *Schwertträger* in the courtyard of the New Reich Chancellery serve as symbols of the mission and aspirations of the *Schutzstaffel*.[150] The torch and the sword, ideology and force, stand as the cornerstones of our struggle for the Reich.

As political soldiers, the National Socialist worldview, the political legacy of our Führer, is our guiding light in this struggle. We have learned from the history of our people and are firmly convinced that the Reich can only be maintained if we keep alive, nurture, and protect the nation's conviction in our shared political mission. The *Schutzstaffel* thus forms a sworn community of fighters, united in good times and bad, committed to upholding the interests of the German Reich and the National Socialist worldview.

---

[149] The *Schutzstaffel* (abbreviated in the original German with the runic symbols ᛋᛋ) was the elite paramilitary corps of the NSDAP, initially formed as Hitler's personal bodyguard but later expanding into a powerful organization tasked with securing the Third Reich both internally and externally and especially with defending the peoples of Europe against the threat of Bolshevism.

[150] The two bronze statues *Fackelträger* ("Torch-bearer") and *Schwertträger* ("Sword-bearer") were commissioned by Albert Speer for the New Reich Chancellery and were cast by Arno Breker in 1939.

FURTHER READING

Beumelburg, Werner. *Bismarck gründet das Reich* ["Bismarck Founds the Reich"]. Oldenburg in Oldenburg: Stalling-Verlag, 1932.

Beumelburg, Werner. *Reich und Rom* ["Reich and Rome"]. Oldenburg in Oldenburg: Stalling-Verlag, 1937.

Chamberlain, Houston Stewart. *Die Grundlagen des neunzehnten Jahrhunderts* ["The Foundations of the Nineteenth Century"]. Munich: Bruckmann Verlag, 1940.

Darré, R. Walther. *Neuordnung unseres Denkens* ["Restructuring Our Way of Thinking"]. Goslar: Verlag Blut und Boden, 1940.

Fahrenkrog, Rolf. *Europas Geschichte als Rassenschicksal* ["Europe's History as a Racial Destiny"]. Leipzig: Hesse und Becker-Verlag, 1937.

Franz, Günther. *Der deutsche Bauernkrieg* ["The German Peasants' War"]. Munich: R. Oldenbourg Verlag, 1939.

Ganzer, Karl Richard. *Das Werden des Reiches* ["The Emerging of the Reich"]. Munich: J. F. Lehmanns Verlag, 1939.

Haller, Johannes. *Die Epochen der deutschen Geschichte* ["The Epochs of German History"]. Stuttgart: Cotta-Verlag, 1940.

Hirsch, Hermann. *Auf steht das Reich gegen Rom* ["The Reich Rises against Rome"]. Stuttgart: Georg Truckenmüller-Verlag,

1940.

Hitler, Adolf. *Mein Kampf.* Munich: Eher-Verlag, 1925.

Huch, Ricarda. *Römisches Reich deutscher Nation* ["Roman Empire of the German Nation"]. Berlin: Atlantis-Verlag, 1934.

Kossinna, Gustaf. *Ursprung und Verbreitung der Germanen in vor- und frühgeschichtlicher Zeit* ["Origin and Dispersal of the Germanic Peoples in Prehistoric Times"]. Leipzig: Kurt Kabitsch-Verlag, 1934.

Krüger, Gerhard. *Geschichte des deutschen Volkes* ["History of the German People"]. Leipzig: Bibliographisches Institut, 1938.

Laasch, Hermann. *Zweitausend Jahre deutschen Geschehens* ["Two Thousand Years of German History"]. Leipzig: Verlag Koehler und Amelang, 1934.

Leers, Johann von. *Entwicklung des Nationalsozialismus von seinem Anfang bis zur Gegenwart* ["Development of National Socialism from its Beginning to the Present"]. Leipzig: Verlag Velhagen und Klasing, 1936.

Leers, Johann von. *Odal, das Lebensgesetz eines ewigen Deutschlands* ["Odal: the Law of Life of an Eternal Germany"]. Goslar: Verlag Blut und Boden, 1935.

Pastenaci, Kurt. *Das Viertausendjährige Reich der Deutschen* ["The Four Thousand Year Old Reich of the Germans"]. Berlin: Nordland-Verlag, 1940.

Sanders, Alexander. *Um die Gestaltung Europas* ["The Shaping of Europe"]. Munich: Hoheneichen-Verlag, 1938.

Schmidt, Friedrich. *Das Reich als Aufgabe* ["The Reich as a Mission"]. Berlin: Nordland-Verlag, 1940.

Stiewe, Friedrich. *Geschichte des deutschen Volkes* ["History of the German People"]. Munich: R. Oldenbourg Verlag, 1940